For our Kids

மனமது செம்மையானால்
இனமது செழிக்கும்

Dr Kaviya Thamizhi

INDIA · SINGAPORE · MALAYSIA

Know Your Kids – For Parents and Teachers

Foreword

Meaning of the book title

I norder to nurture healthy and happy children, we must understand the mind and the thought process of the society we are living in. When the mind is encouraged to be happy and sovereign, we evolve and flourish as a species.

To explain this concept, we need to understand who we are and how our society has come to be what it is today. Here, we need to explore the meaning and identity of "Thamizh", which will form the conceptual foundation for the future of whole of humanity.

தமிழ் என்றால் என்ன? தமிழன் என்பவன் யார்?

நாம் யார் என்ற கேள்விக்கு பதில் கிடைத்து விட்டாலே பல மனம் சார்ந்த பிரச்சனைகளிலிருந்து விடுபட்டுவிடலாம்.

தமிழ் என்ற சொல் – தம் + இழ் என்ற இரண்டு சொற்களால் ஆனது.

தம் என்றால் "என்னுடைய" என்று பொருள்.

இழ் என்பது "இறையாண்மையை" குறிக்கும்.

இதற்கு அர்த்தம் –

என் வாழ்க்கையை என் விருப்பம் போல் நான் வாழ்ந்துகொள்வேன், நான் யாருக்கும் அடிமையாய் இருக்க மாட்டேன், யாரையும் அடிமைப்படுத்தவும் மாட்டேன். எனக்கும் என்னைச் சார்ந்தவர்களுக்கும் எது நல்லது என்பதை நானே தீர்மானித்துக் கொள்வேன்.

எனக்கும் என்னைச் சார்ந்தவர்களுக்கும் நன்மை பயக்கும் வகையில் யாரேனும் நடந்து கொண்டால் அவர் வேறு மொழி பேசுபவராக இருந்தாலும் நான் அவரையும் என் இனத்தாரை போலவே அன்புடனும் மரியாதையுடனும் நடத்துவேன்.

Hence it has been proven beyond doubt, that the identity of "Thamizh" people is not confined to the language they speak, not confined to the land area they live in, but it encompasses the ideology of the people, irrespective of caste, creed, color, language etc.

தமிழ் என்பது ஒரு மொழியின் அடையாளம் மட்டும் அல்ல, அது ஒரு சித்தாந்தத்தின் அடையாளம்.

தமிழின் நோக்கம் ஒரு மனிதனை சிந்திக்க வைப்பது.

How to promote this healthy and authentic style of thinking?

It is not going to simply happen by praying or just reading a few good books. It takes persistent effort by the society to nurture healthy minds right from a child's birth.

This book has dealt in detail on child rearing practices from a psychiatrist's and sociologist's perspective that will help our schools and parents alike to build healthy and happy children who are capable of independent thinking.

Within few years of following the principles laid out in this book, we will be able to see a dramatic change in the mentality of our children and Tamilnadu will soon become the forefront of quality education provider to the world.

Our own educational institutions will become the next "Harvard" or even better!

Acknowledgement

I want to thank my mother – whom I have hated most of my life because of the preconceived notions and the values that this malformed society instilled in me. It took me more than 3 decades of life to realise that my Mother is an absolute Angel and a Hero to be worshipped. Her sacrifices and the sufferings she endured are unmatchable. My mom deserves everything this world has to offer and a little more than that. I dedicate this book to my Mother – the woman who made it all happen. She handled it all and gave us a life which nobody else from her background could give to their kids. If not for her, I would have been pining for all the material things and been on an unending journey to find myself all the while losing myself. My mom is the magic I have wanted and I wish her the best in her life and all the happiness that one could experience. Understanding my mom has made me trust the universe more. Maybe you too should. If you want to heal, just understand your parents' perspective, because most of your problems stem from your childhood and if you are not at peace with your past, you will never be happy in your present or the future.

I love you Miya! And I am terribly sorry for all my stinging words... You don't deserve it.

I request all the readers to wish love and health on all the mothers in the world as they read this.

My sincerest thanks to my "Daddy Dearest" for his patience and tolerance towards me.

I owe every meaningful second of my life to my baby "Ammu" for giving me a reason to wake up every morning.

My sincere thanks and gratitude to my beacon of light – Professor Dr Thirunavukkarasu, for just being the man that he is.

Why This Book?

$\mathbf{M}$ental health issues are on the rise and nobody seems to be "The mental health" of the kids of today's world. The parents are entangled in their own problems and they are trying to give their children everything they themselves didn't have as kids back in their days. So, this gives them the illusion that their children's lives are better than their lives and that the kids these days do not have any problem. On the contrary, the children are burdened with a lot more problems than their ancestors had in the past. Because the world that exists today did not exist before and hence this new world has its own new set of problems and solutions to which most of us are blind.

Mental health disturbances have their roots deeply set in childhood and it is mostly the childhood traumas and thinking style that shows up itself in later years as mental illnesses. In order to prevent the evolution of mental health issues, we will have to delve deeply into the minds of children and try to build resilient little beings. There is a saying, "A stitch in time saves nine".

"காணி சோம்பல் ஊரு பாழ்".

If we fail to address the emotional needs of kids today, we might have to pay a bigger price for it later.

A small word of care and support in kindergarten can prevent a Major Depressive Disorder in the thirties. It may sound implausible but studies show that happy children have successful career and harmonious family lives in the future. I have heard many patients in their twenties lament that, "If only someone had told me that it will all be okay, I would've avoided a lot of hardships".

"எல்லாம் சரி ஆயிடும், பாத்துக்கலாம் என்று கூறி சாய்வதற்கு ஒரு தோள்".

Children get to spend a good 6-8 hours of the day in schools and most of their productive parts of the day are in the vicinity of teachers and friends. Parents do have a role but it is not as much important as they think it is. A teacher's role in a child's life is more valuable to a child than a parent, because a good teacher can help the child tide over through a rough home situation but a good mother cannot be a teacher that a child needs or wants. I am here not undermining the role of parents but just trying to point out the fact that children tend to learn faster under the guidance of a good teacher.

"A lucky student is one, he/she who has found a mentor for life".

"உனக்கான ஆசானை நீ கண்டுகொண்டுவிட்டால் நீ பாக்கியசாலி".

A teacher has more time to observe the child and get a better understanding of what the child is going through because children tend to grow closer to people whom they are in proximity with. For example, most best friends are children who sat next to each other on the same bench. Your best friend may be the person who sat next to you in your yoga class. *Proximity* is one of the factors that play an important role in making and building relationships. In this context, parents drop their children at school, feed them, and put them to bed. So, this amounts to only a small percentage of the twenty-four hours in a day.

A lot of subjects are covered in the teacher training courses throughout the world but the mental health needs of a child are not described as much. When children or in general people are happy, they tend to be more productive, more creative and happier. Childhood has been drafted in civilization as a major learning phase and hence it is pertinent that we make children happy to enhance their potential.

When you're in a position to take care of the others, (here – children), it is important to be able to take care of yourself first. A bleeding and injured person cannot donate blood, likewise an unhappy teacher or a parent cannot understand the mental health needs of a child lest make a child happy. If you are a teacher and if you think life has been cruel to you, it is necessary to cure your wounds first before you deal with little minds that need nurturing. Refer to my previous book, "Buy Happiness from a Bookshelf", for your own mental health care needs so that you can understand yourself and develop empathy. Empathy is the main tool to explore minds. If you think you're burned out or if your life is exhausting you, then you will not have the energy to empathise. Being empathetic is demanding and energy draining but can be heart fulfilling if you put it to good use and create a smile in a distressed being. Teachers definitely have a lot to take care of – their own children and family. As far as I know, most teachers are underpaid and overworked. It is important to take care of your mental health first. This will help you to be a good teacher, which in turn will make you love your job, in turn reducing the meaninglessness of life. Not everyone can become a good teacher. The mind has to be trained in a certain way to harness the exact nature of good teachers.

Once you're all set, I welcome you to this amazing ride into young minds. Being a teacher comes with immense responsibility of creating minds. Not every job has this novel power. Teaching is a powerful profession. With power, comes responsibility. Let us all be responsible human beings. We're all teachers in one way or another, though not professionally.

Parents have learned to juggle work and family life. But family life to a parent means meeting the basic needs of a child and the time that they get to spend on exploring the mental make up a child is relatively lesser due to current day work-life situation.

If we cater to the children of today, we can build strong citizens for our country within the next 5-10 years and a lot of mental health disturbances can be eradicated within a few generations.

This book will hold good for the next 20 years, after which there will be other pressing issues and changes in the psychological make up which will need newer methods, learnings and teachings.

What are those changes going to be – only time will tell.

For example – 100 years ago, no one would have imagined that tonnes of cooked food will be dumped in garbage as remnants from fancy weddings because at that time malnutrition was rampant in the country with many kids being grossly under-weight, as opposed to the current scenario where 1 in 5 kids are obese.

Mind and mental health keep advancing itself according to the parallel developments in science and technology and hence we must keep ourselves updated. Learning has no limits. Mental health professionals' opinions must be sought periodically and also as and when necessary for drafting regional/national educational policies.

Normal Development

When most mammals are born, they gain the ability to get on their own feet within very few days of birth. But human babies, unfortunately or fortunately, are born with a lot of limitations. They cannot survive on their own. This is because the human brain (especially prefrontal cortex) that developed the capability of enormous growth compared to the other mammals makes it difficult for the baby to be delivered through the mother's pelvis if left to attain its maximal growth inside the womb. In other words, if the brain attains full maturity while inside the pelvis, then the BIG brain that has developed will not be able to come out of the mother's pelvis. Hence the baby is delivered before the brain has the capacity to function fully.

The most important period of development for the child is the first 1000 days or roughly the first three years of life. It is during these years, the child learns how to see, walk, talk, understand the environment etc. This is also the period when the mind develops the subconscious. You may not remember remembering many events from childhood but you may just know them. This is because these things are stored in the "subconscious" part of the brain and influences the functioning of the conscious parts of the brain until death. Having a healthy "subconscious" brain is important to have an intelligent and happy brain in adulthood. Some studies say that memory area in the brain is not formed until three years of age but it is debatable. Children who have begun training in sports like swimming, yoga or martial arts or music from 2 years of age have turned out to be stalwarts in their respective fields. This proves that lessons etched in the subconscious brain have longer lasting impacts than the lessons that were learnt by the conscious adult brain. It is at this phase, the brain learns to differentiate between shapes, colors and make sense of three-dimensional images. This is why we have to spend more time and effort to give toddlers a healthy vibrant environment to grow.

The mistakes that we do

In this period, the child learns to differentiate between a behaviour that is appreciated and a behaviour that leads to punishment and scolding. An unattended child will fail to make the differentiation and do whatever it wants. The nervous system in the body (brain and other nerves) develops a sheet of tissue called the myelin sheath around the nerve fibres during early developmental days. Because this is incomplete during birth, babies need much care and attention from the parents. When the baby starts moving, (like crawling, grasping objects, walking, running, grabbing things, eating, etc) the baby learns the relationship between free will and control.

When the baby learns a behaviour, for example, that moving legs consecutively in small steps result in walking- the baby gains control of a part of the brain that is responsible for such a movement. It is important in the first three years to let the baby explore as much bodily movements as possible because the mind and body are connected, and when one gains control of finer body movements, they can be taught to control the functioning of the mind in later years. It is difficult to talk to a toddler about feelings and mind. But it is easier to teach them movements because body is a three-dimensional figure that the baby can comprehend. Soon, the baby learns to explore the environment using all the senses namely – taste, smell, sound, touch, vision. Some Eastern scriptures say that "The Third Eye" can be activated if children practice yoga as soon as they learn to walk. The Western analogy of this context would be the Pineal Gland that is active in younger age, (which is regarded as the third eye) tends to calcify as one gets older. Hence, in CT brain scans of older people a calcified pineal gland can be seen. This means that the Pineal Gland (Third Eye) which is present (and possibly active) in children tends to calcify (and become inactive) in adults. It has been shown that in some people who practice yoga and martial arts, this Pineal Gland is found to be present even in old age. The exact function of this Pineal Gland is still under research.

Toddlers, as they grow will be exploring the environment using different senses as each sense organ matures. As children are fed right from birth, they learn to explore things by putting them into their mouth. This is the reason why kids place everything in thier mouth as they try to experience the new object. Then, the exploration of things by breaking objects into its smaller parts tend to dominate the senses. The touch sense is important to developing resilience because the feeling of warmth provided by the parents/primary caregiver increases the secretion of a chemical called "oxytocin" which builds a sense of connection and a feeling of safety.

Why is oxytocin important?

This chemical prevents the development of certain mental health disturbances like psychosis, reduces the risk of developing suicidal thoughts etc.

How to increase the production of oxytocin?

Lend out lavish hugs, cuddles and kisses to your child.

Parents want their kids to learn as much information as possible right from a younger age and they end up spoiling the kids with the so called commercially marketed educational toys and smart phone applications. At this age, the most important part of the brain to develop is the part of the brain that controls what we call "The Mind". Children may not be able to understand the subtle emotions but they master the concepts of reward and punishment even without explanation.

Any behaviour that is rewarded consistently with praise is likely to be repeated and a behaviour that is punished is likely to fade away. The trick here is to make the child understand that a particular behaviour is rewarded. In order to convey this, the reward must be something that the child appreciates. It could be a kiss, a cuddle, a piece of cake, applause, or anything that makes sense to the child. Likewise, the punishment can be ignoring the behaviour, saying "No", or removing the source that caused the behaviour.

It is not necessary to express your love for your child by showering them with all the toys in the world. If your child has everything they know, then the process of imagination comes down. For example, when you show a Dinosaur picture/toy to a child, the child sees what it is and every time the word Dinosaur pops up, the child remembers that image of the Dinosaur that was shown. But if a child has only heard the word "Dinosaur" and has never seen it, then the child begins to create an image of the dinosaur in its mind. This is how creativity begins. The idea is not about buying or not buying a Dinosaur toy, but to give the child some time to think about it without overloading them with information. When you have all the answers already, the need for thinking becomes zero. The memorized answers will be retrieved from the memory centre directly. It is important to stimulate the growing mind to constantly think and decipher solutions.

Having a peer circle is important right from toddler age. This is to make the child understand that he/she is not the only child in this universe. Some parents are particular about making their entire family revolve around their kid at home and this is a very dangerous style of upbringing that I am seeing in the recent days.

Your child is just like any other child and this message must be clear to the child so it prevents problems in future relationships and career. Every child is special but parents have this feeling that their child is extra special. There is no one who is extra special.

Children tend to show their areas of interest as early as three years of age and if parents are perceptive enough, that particular area of interest can be nurtured and cultivated for future prospects.

Everyone loves the smell of earth after a rain. Ever wondered why?

This is because of the bacteria – Actinomycetes in the soil that undergo an enzymatic reaction produce a chemical, "Geosmin" that causes this smell. Studies have shown that this bacteria increases our immunity and causes an increase in the secretion of "Serotonin" in the brain. Serotonin is the neurochemical that gives us the feeling of "Happiness". Children love playing with sand and they always tend to dig earth when left unattended. This behaviour is soothing as it activates the calming part of brain thereby reducing aggression and irritability. It is not advisable to restrain children from playing with sand all the time as long as they are supervised and in safe conditions. This also improves creativity as sand is like an abstract toy and children can learn to experiment with their surroundings.

Happy Children

Happy children come not only from happy homes but also from troubled homes. So don't blame yourself for all that is happening in your child's life and mind. Nobody has any clue as to why exactly some children are happy and why some children are irritable and labile. We have data from studies that were conducted in many households across different countries that all came up with some uniform family characteristics where children were difficult to manage.

Such family characteristics include (but not limited to) the following:

1. Families with domestic violence.
2. Either of the parent having a drug abuse problem.
3. Single child.
4. Living in isolation where both parents are working and child is left without a carer.
5. Physical abuse.
6. Strict parenting – setting rules that are inappropriate, setting high standards for children.
7. Families with single father. (Apparently, children of single mothers were scored to be high in emotional intelligence).

8. Narcissism in either of the parents. (Parents who prioritized their own well-being to their children and made the kids feel inadequate and not worthy of love and affection).
9. Mental illness in either parent where the children have to take up the role of the adult.
10. Families with frequent marital discord.
11. Poverty.

Some life situations may be inevitable (தவிர்க்க முடியாத). Giving birth to a child comes with a long-term responsibility. Every individual has a right to marry and procreate but bringing up a child must be a conscious decision that the parent has to make. It is the duty of both the parents and the society to ensure that our children are safe, have all their physical, emotional, and social needs met. It is pertinent for all the parents to consider all relevant factors and circumstances before having a child. The child does not owe a parent anything. Do not expect your child to meet your emotional needs. Let the child be a child and live freely in this beautiful world.

The Kindergarten

It is not uncommon for many schools in developing countries to start enrolling children as early as 4 years of age. The average age of enrolment of children in school is much higher in the developed countries like Finland, Sweden, America etc.

Indian schools have the system where all schools irrespective of the fee structure expect their students to wear school uniforms to bring a sense of oneness to the kids. I am writing this chapter in the context of the school atmosphere in India. Children are forced to wear clothes that are made of polyester and shoes with socks all the year round. Here specific mention goes to "all the year round" because in the southern parts of India, it is summer all year around. We are still following what the British taught us. It is reasonable to wear shirts with collars, tight shoes and socks in London, but wearing that in Indian summer is absolute non-sense.

Wearing uniforms is one of the means to eliminate discrimination and hence it has become an absolute necessity in the Indian community but the material in which it is stitched should be climate friendly.

This kindergarten period is the age where the bones "Develop and Align" so they together form a good frame for the muscles and organs to grow. Unfortunately, the kids are made to sit in chairs for hours together which is a very bad posture for the body to be in, for most of the day. Children must be involved in as much physical activity as possible from kindergarten to middle school age. Physical activity in kindergarten should not be provided in the form of a structured physical activity but instead should be an informal one where groups of children get together and create games with their own set of rules and regulations. Apart from this, it is essential to find out special interests that each child has.

Teachers tend to say things like "pin drop silence", "no talking" to kids.

On the contrary, kids should be encouraged talk. Speech center is most developed in humans and it would be a shame to not put it to good use. We have to encourage children to talk to each other and share whatever they have in their minds. THIS IS WHERE THE KINDERGARTEN SCHOOLS HAVE FAILED.

It is essential for the teacher to identify that one particular child who does not speak as much or that child who does not socialize as much. Such children need special attention and we have to explore what the child is going through at home to be able to help the child. Promoting verbal communication from 1 year of age will improve the overall intelligence of the child to a great extent. Testing a child's speaking ability will be an easy way to identify a child who is going through a tough time. Children may not be vocal with their problems. They are mostly the silent sufferers. If you find a silent kid in the room, please pay attention. Even introverts become extroverts around the right people. Being a teacher entails not only teaching, but also identifying which child needs help.

The child who shows up in an unkempt manner, crying all the time, and looks anxious definitely has something else going on. All cries are not cry for help but we'd rather not miss any cry because we do not know which cry is a cry for help.

Any child with unexplained injuries, overtly sexualized behaviour must be promptly reported and attended to. Many teachers tend to blame the kids for their disruptive behaviour. Children are only reacting to their environment and we have to study the environment they are in, in order to understand them.

Temper Tantrums

No parent or teacher will be thrilled by the title of this chapter. Every child throws a tantrum (கோப வெறித்தனங்கள்) atleast once a month.

Why does this happen?

1. Most common cause is when a child's need is not met.
2. When parents don't give a convincing reason as to why a child's want is denied.
3. When a child is hungry.
4. Constipation or urinary tract infection.
5. Any recent changes in medications that the child is taking.
6. Recent changes at home or school about which the child was not properly prepared for.
7. Wearing too tight or uncomfortable clothes which may increase the overall tendency to be irritable.
8. When parents have always been yielding to every request of the child and then they suddenly seem unavailable and have become strict.
9. Sometimes, when there is a fight among a group of kids, the kid who was hurt more than the others throws a tantrum to gain attention and seek justice.

How to deal with such situations?

<u>Things to do at that moment:</u>

Try to reason with the kid. Have a conversation in a normal tone of your voice and let the child know that you expect the same from your child in return. "If you keep crying while talking, I may never be able to understand what you're saying", this usually helps. Telling a wailing kid to calm down will never help. It could make the situation worse. It is necessary to be very calm and composed yourself while handling a child throwing a tantrum. Very often, we tend to get agitated and impatient. This will snowball into a bigger problem than the original one at hand and things may go south. Take a deep breath and ascertain yourself that it is not going to be easy. It is like entering a battle field knowing pretty well you're going to lose yet all you want is peace and not victory.

The children want to win. Your job here is to calm them down, help them overcome the irritable mood and make them believe that you are working under their will and control. If you try to dominate, the already helpless child will feel more helpless which in turn will make the child want to yell and scream more.

When the mind is agitated, the power of reasoning (பகுத்தறிவு) comes to a halt.

"ஆத்திரகாரனுக்கு புத்தி மட்டு".

A calm mind can think of infinite solutions. There are going to be a lot of back and forth reasons and promises in the conversation between you and your child but make sure you are aware of what you're promising in return for desirable behaviour because all your promises will be recorded and used against you in forthcoming problematic situations.

This is a rough idea on how to deal with a difficult child but it depends on a lot of factors and each kid has its own set of agendas and hence there is no one uniform solution to deal with all kids. Each child needs a very personalized approach. Please read the following and brainstorm with your child, of course only when your child is in a good mood. If your child is not able to communicate as much, then try to understand the situations and analyse the tantrums retrospectively.

Study ABC

Whenever you are trying to solve a problem, the primary aim must be to understand the problem.

Learn the antecedents

What happened just before the tantrum that drove the child to become irritable? What are the triggers? Are the triggering events the same every time or is it a new trigger today? Was the child hungry?

What about the trigger the child did not like or is finding difficult to cope up with?

Does the child have a control over the trigger? Or is the child being a passive victim to the triggering offense?

Is the triggering event related to any particular person? If yes, then who is this person and why is the child scared about this person?

While devising answers to these set of questions, we will be able to understand the child better and get a hint of the child's likes and dislikes as well. So analysing the antecedents tells us not only about the temper tantrum, but also few more secrets about the child's personality. If possible try to find answers to these –

What is the trigger?

Why did the trigger occur and why was the child triggered by it?

How did it happen?

When did the event occur?

Where did the tantrum occur?

The above western theory on studying and understanding a behavior has already been explained by our own Thiruvalluvar:

"நோய்நாடி நோய்முதல் நாடி அதுதணிக்கும்
வாய்நாடி வாய்ப்பச் செயல்".

Learn the behaviour

Most commonly, children tend to display specific bodily movements and crying in response to triggering situations. They have a typical set of words and movements that occur during each episode. What is important here is to make sure that the child does not hurt itself or the others while displaying disappointments. Some kids have the habit of throwing objects like the phone, the tv remote etc. onto the triggering person or may try smashing them as a result of expressing anger.

Observe the behaviour like a third person. Don't get overtly emotional nor take it personal. It is not entirely your fault when your child behaves in socially inappropriate ways. Some kids just lie on the ground, irrespective of where they are and refuse to get up until they get what they want. As a parent you may have umpteen responsibilities and chores to attend to and you may be in a hurry. At these situations, you have two choices.

(i) To budge to whatever the child demands so you can move on with your next chore, which will give the child a bad example and lesson and a tendency to repeat it in the future, or

(ii) Stay with the child. Tell the child just once and calmly that – the child's demands are too unrealistic and that you can settle for something less or none at all depending on the situation you are dealing with. This may cost you a few important hours of the day but this way of handling the situation makes the tantrum less likely to be repeated in the future. You can walk proudly with the satisfaction that you are bringing up a healthy, responsible and a reasonable child into this world.

If you find them doing anything that would harm them or the others, move the kid to a safer environment and let the child continue with the behaviour. Soon, the child reaslises that this behaviour does not have any effect on you and slowly stops the adamancy and moves past it. Some parents feel ashamed when their children shout or scream in public. When you decided to have a child, you actually signed up for all of this. It is part of the package. This is nothing to feel ashamed about and even if people judge you of being a bad parent, it is not your business to worry about the other people. You made a commitment to have a child and you have to deal with them through thick and thin. Parents and teachers who have their proud moments when their children/students excel in curricular or extra-curricular activities should be aware that such desirable behaviour will not exist without a few undesirable behaviour. It is okay to have our children throw a tantrum occasionally. A child becoming angry and agitated occasionally is also a sign of healthy development as it is a reflection of the "I will fight for what I believe in" feeling inside.

Kids are a bundle of emotions and challenges. They are just learning to explore the world and deal with emotions, failures and rejections. Even adults don't handle failures well. So, it is very understandable when children throw a fuss every now and then.

Study the consequence

Children learn from the consequence of their tantrums and depending on that they decide whether they can use it to their benefit or not.

The most important part of the consequence is, "How you react towards them". Parents tend to shower their love on a child throwing a tantrum and cajole the child to calm down.

But is it healthy?

At the end of a tantrum- if the needs of the child are met- the brain wires the tantrum behaviour strongly and this circuit gets activated every time a need is not met. The child wins.

But if the needs of the child are not met but replaced with a more reasonable outcome, then the child learns that he/she is not the center of the universe and that the universe does not revolve around them. They learn that their tantrum behaviour does not have any beneficial effect. With the power of reasoning, come men of great power and position. When a child learns to reason out things and explain their needs and desires in acceptable ways, then they can wade through life with ease and joy. This circuit – The Cognitive Circuit – where "THINKING" predominates, helps children evolve at a much higher frequency than the others. Most successful scientists have mastered the art of using the cognitive circuit and not succumbing to the emotional circuit.

Emotions form a screen in front of our thinking mind and influence our thoughts based on that emotion thereby preventing us from accessing the reality in which the world exists.

<u>World exists in two forms:</u>

1. One – is its real existence and

2. The other – is the image of the world that we have made in our minds with our own life experiences and emotions.

In order to understand the world, we will have to break out of our emotions and preconceived thoughts and see the world for what it is. Reasoning is one of the important first steps to understand the world. This behaviour is difficult to learn and practice but when it is once mastered there is no going back. Reasoning also helps prevent the onset of depression, anxiety, drug abuse, etc. in later life. In fact, one of the talking therapies (psychotherapy) that we prescribe for various mental health disorders includes the concept of educating patients to master the art of reasoning which will enable them to change the way they think (creating a new style of thinking).

EVR Periyar was one of the earliest social psychotherapists in India, who helped to reduce the social illnesses by inculcating the power of "Reasoning", or "பகுத்தறிவு". In psychiatry we use this same concept used by Periyar to help people reason out their emotions so they can understand their life better and it is one of the effective treatment methods to treat depression, anxiety, OCD etc.

How to reduce tantrums?

Once we deal with a single episode of tantrum, we must be cautious because there is going to be another episode of increased or decreased severity depending on the way the tantrum was received in its first episode.

In order to prevent such episodes from happening-make a detailed study of the behaviour and try addressing each issue. The safety of the child must be borne in mind at all costs.

Case report

(i) This is an incident that I witnessed when I went to a school to deliver a speech during the school's Annual Cultural Function. As I was waiting to be seated, I saw a girl child roughly 6-7 years old, with her mother just across the stage in its right end behind the curtains. This child was throwing a tantrum, I didn't know why, she was throwing her arms and legs up in the air, wailing at the top of her lungs. Knowing the Indian culture like the back of my hand, I was waiting for the mother to lose her cool, pick up the child and move to a space where her tantrums couldn't be heard or even worse to slap her. Instead, she just sat there beside her, scrolling her phone paying no heed whatsoever to this child. Within a few minutes, (I was aware of the time because that is the time it took for the host to get the guests seated) the child stopped crying, and caught hold of her mother's hands and moved towards where the crowd was seated. This divine woman was continuing to exist in her serene tranquility. A lesson to learn from here is – children mirror our emotions. They are perceptive to everything from a minor flinch in our voice to the slightest grimace in our face. They almost always reciprocate the emotions of their primary caretakers/parents. This is the best method to deal with a child overwhelmed with emotions. Just like adults, if they are given the time to experience and process their emotions, they would be just fine. If this was met with precocious curbing of their behaviour by force, these emotions would be stored in their mind-body system, and would have a tendency to be repeated on future occasions. When an emotion is not processed, the learning does not happen. Such children grow up to become fussy, unable to deal with authority figures, unable to take a firm stand, and regress to childlike behaviour when faced with difficult life circumstances during adult life as well. Unprocessed emotions make the children repeat the same mistakes over and over again. From this event, the child would have learnt that creating a scene in public is not going to get her anywhere. Such lessons learned in childhood have prevented people from becoming emotionally incontinent in later life. It is those kinds of people whom we tend to call "wise", or "cool" For example, our cricket captain, MS Dhoni. Such people have more friends, are successful in their career because when you're in control of your emotions, you think with more clarity and make wiser decisions.

(ii) He was an 8-year-old boy, Ram. He was fine until kindergarten. His problems started when he was moved to this new school to study first standard. He made it impossible for his mother to convince him to go to school. She had tried star charts, behaviour modification techniques but none of it seemed to work. Over the last few weeks, he has been very disruptive at school, trying to hurt the other kids, calling them names, stealing little things and this kind of attitude was highly unlikely of him. The teacher complained to the mother that Ram was an exemplary kid in the initial few days of school but later he has been acting really out of character. Then she came to see me in desperation as she was worried that Ram may never go to school and become a failure in life. The boy would throw things, break household articles, yell at his mom and off late he has started hurting himself whenever the topic of school was discussed. His mother had threatened him that she would enroll him in a residential school if he continued to behave this way. Hearing this, he left home and never returned that night. He was found wandering in the railway station by the local police and was brought home. As I explored further, I learnt that his old school (the kindergarten school) was near his home and that he would walk to his school every day. He was happy about going to school. He had seemed to be a cheerful kid while in kindergarten, but the new school was quite far away from his home and he had to take the school van. His parents could not afford to have a vehicle of their own and hence found it convenient to send him to school in the school van. They had made it clear that he should not miss the van timings and they were strict about this rule. I conducted 2 one-on-one sessions with Ram and with his mother's permission I carried out a physical examination and found out that Ram has been sexually abused. His mother had taught that bleeding was because Ram had constipation as he had not been eating properly. This news shattered his mother. On gentle questioning, Ram revealed that his van driver did things to him that he didn't like and that the driver threatened to kill him if he said about this to anybody else. The relevant authorities were informed and his mother was broken to hear this because all along she has been blaming Ram for his behaviour and she felt guilty for not being able to understand him and his problems. I took Ram into therapy and now he is doing well in school and specifically interested in swimming. When your child displays unusual behaviour, it is important to analyse and understand the origin of such behaviour before trying to find solutions. If you have difficulty comprehending a certain situation, please seek professional help. This does not mean that you are incompetent as a parent, instead it shows how involved you are as a parent. Nobody said parenting was easy!

Devise a star chart

A star chart is a popular method to help children develop healthy behaviours over a period of time. It entails the process of marking a star in the chart for every positive or desirable behaviour that the child exhibits. We can make a deal with the children as to they would get a treat or a gift when they earn 5 stars. The rewarding treat or gift must be something that the child likes. This way we can promote healthy behaviour in children. The star chart also works the other way round, in the sense that a star can be removed when the child exhibits a disruptive or an unhealthy behaviour. The important rules to be followed while using a star chart are:-

1. It has to be consistent.
2. No amending rules once they are set.
3. No exceptions during special occasions or birthdays.
4. Strict adherence despite your difficult work schedule.
5. The reward may change over time because children evolve faster than adults and hence their likes and dislikes may change. Teachers and parents must be perceptive to such changes and reward appropriately.

6. It takes a considerably long period of time for a behaviour to be established, altered or removed. So, patience is the key. Do not expect results overnight.

Don't play good Cop/bad Cop

When attempting to change a particular behaviour in a child, it is important for all the members in the house to comply with the same set of rules and follow the same approach when dealing with a problem behaviour.

One day, a twelve years old boy was brought to my clinic as he had been refusing to go to school for the past 6 months. On speaking to him for 3 sessions, he slowly opened up to me saying that his Thamizh teacher had scolded him for bad handwriting. Since then, he has been staying home, playing, and his grandparents who are also living with him were keeping him engaged throughout the day by giving him money for snacks and letting him use their smart phone. Then I counselled the mother about the do's and don't's, taught her the principles of behaviour modification and asked her to review after 2 weeks.

She came after 2 weeks disgruntled and said, "He is still not going to school". She expressed her inability to correct this behaviour as the patient's grandparents were not letting her implement any of the rules I had suggested.

When I asked her why she was not able to voice out her justifiable cause against them, she said, "My husband does not have a job. My father-in-law is the sole bread winner of the family. Even now we are living off his pension. So, I can't voice out my opinions. They even feed my kid whatever he asks for like chips, chocolates, biscuits etc. I tell them it is not healthy but they don't listen to me".

In this case, the mother has complete understanding of the situation but is in a helpless position to make a change because her family is dependent upon her in-laws for basic survival. Another reason why she keeps putting up with this family scenario is because she is not educated enough to get a job and is financially and socially dependent upon her in-laws. Her husband on the other hand has proved to be useless as a father and as a husband. In the Indian community, it is still a practice where women are not educated and are married off to a guy who seeks the least dowry. This mother is a victim of social inequality, and a prisoner of her circumstances which she had no control over.

The first step in the treatment of this kid is to help his mother get a job and earn her living so she need not be a modern slave to her in-laws. Once she becomes financially independent, her confidence is boosted and with that she makes her voice heard loud and clear, improving the status of herself and that of her family.

Another aspect that we need to shed light on here is – the inconsistency among family members in treating a child where a change in behavoiur is warranted. The grandparents have made this 6 months a heaven for this kid by giving him all the junk foods to eat, a smart phone – making him an ideal couch potato.

Here the kid sees the mother as the Villain – because she is trying to correct his behaviour by taking the phone away from him, and refuses to give him junk food.

He sees his grandparents as his Hero because they give him everything he asks for immediately without foreseeing the consequences.

Sometimes either of the parents or grandparents (here), play to be a good parent by complying to the child's demands so they may be liked more by their child. This will prove counter productive because we are teaching the kid that a person becomes more likeable if we give them whatever they demand for. This will get translated as, "In future if somebody else gets me what I want then my loyalty will shift from you to this other person". In such instances, the kids may like you only for what you give and not for the health promoting intentions you have for them. They will not know the value of people and will not give importance to virtues instead focus on material things thereby losing touch with humanity. Such kids may grow on to become intense manipulators perfecting the art of becoming a narcissist.

Another point that we will have to discuss is why the Thamizh teacher scolded him. It was because of bad handwriting.

Now I request you all to take a second to think, how much of messages or text content in life are we writing by hand? It is NIL for most of the human population. Writing by hands may become obsolete in the next few years to come as everything is digitalized, thanks to digital India. More emphasis must be given to learning new information and exploring new faculties that interest the self than on improving handwriting that has zero returns for the future.

The Fussy Kid

First of all, accept the fact that you have a fussy kid in hand. It is not going to be easy. The child is going to be demanding. Some kids have a list of things they like and don't like. When the dislike list is too long, then I'm afraid to break the truth- that you have a fussy kid. It is okay to not like a lot of things. The problem arises when the child tries deliberately to avoid everything and every person that the child dislikes. At such situations – it is necessary to explain that we will have to do certain things even if we don't like them. Even adults do. It would help better if you could show an analogy from your own life. For example, "I don't like going to work, but I have to work anyway just so I can pay for our food and shelter. This is how life works".

We will have to normalize the notion that humans do things that they don't like just because they are obligated to do so. It is not that difficult to explain this concept to kids because the words – "like" and "don't like" are prevalent among kids from a young age, around one year of age. Children who are younger and less vocal than the others may not get this point, but with practice they can be made to catch this. Understanding the nature of behaviour and modifying them using star charts will help deal with fussy kids in general.

Parents of the Kindergarteners:

As glamorous and luring it may seem, some parents who are trying to live their dreams through their children turn their kids into young fashion models and find great pride and confidence in doing so. Such exposure to young children may definitely boost their economic pockets but it will certainly drain their intellectual pockets.

This means the focus of the kids will shift

> **From** the outer world and exploration -
> **To** the sense of beauty of the physical body.

Staying fit is necessary but not to the extent of instilling the concept and ideals of adult standards of beauty in children. Over time such kids will cease to see the others and self for the inner expensive virtues such as kindness, compassion, loyalty, trust etc. Instead their assessment of another person's worth will be reduced to the way they look and the latest trendy clothes that they wear. They will begin to harbour values of what we call "Histrionic Personality". This personality is the one where people show shallow emotions and form superficial fake relationships and refuse to acknowledge the inner beauty, which will impair all their future relationships with significant ones (spouse, their own children etc.).

At a very young age if children are exposed to the glitz and glam of show business, they will learn that the value of a person is assessed on the spotlessness of their skin and the so called "good looking" facial features. Once this learning is established in their minds, it is difficult to help them unlearn. Children learn more by observing than from preaching/teaching.

Some parents may be of the opinion that – let the kids walk the ramp for now, later I will teach them all these values. This is not a healthy way of teaching. This will induce a conflicted pattern of thoughts in the kids' minds because we are teaching them the contrary, i.e., we are showing in hard core proof with evidence that their value is based on looks – something that these kids learn through practical implementation and then when we teach them the exact opposite of it (that looks don't matter), they are provided with two contradictory thoughts. It is pertinent to note here that any lesson has its greatest impact when learnt through practical approach.

Also, when parents teach kids something that is exactly the opposite of what they have learnt through practical experience, the kids learn that their parents are not knowledgeable enough and slowly begin to lose value for their parents' words. Once the value is lost, – respect, trust and love are also lost in succession.

It is criminal to deprive the kids of their childhood and make them feel like a teenager from a tender age. The best part of being a child is "not knowing". The joy that comes with innocence and naivety is insurmountable. The developing brain is starved of experiences and as adults it is our duty to give our kids healthy experiences and nurture their brains to become resilient. One may question, "Then what about the other kids who start fashion modelling since a young age?". That is someone else's problem, not yours! They will realise the wrath of it after ten years.

At this age, the sense of gender develops, but it is limited to plays and toys. Girls and boys don't think much about gender or differentiate into their genders much. So they get along with each other better than they would in middle school. Girls don't get the sense of "womanhood" or "lady-like" until their early teens and into early adulthood. At this age, they are just kids. Likewise boys don't get "masculine" or "chivalrous", they too are still kids. This lack of profound awareness to social rules and obligations makes them oblivious to physical appearances and entails the sense of "child-ness" into them, which makes the entire experience of childhood worthwhile. If you are a 90s kid, imagine how happy you were when you actually believed peacock's plumage will deliver babies in your notebook and fed it with pencil shavings? How carefree were you when you thought that cricketer Ricky Ponting used a spring bat to win that World Cup?

Can you imagine kids of these days coming up with such ridiculous theories? Absolutely No. Because everything is out there in the open for them to see and learn. They learn quickly and understand easily. Is this beneficial or will this hasty life lead on to dire consequences? Only time will answer.

Food and Sleep

Mothers get really anxious about their kids' nutrition. According to them, their child should eat according to their (the mother's) own satiety and not according to the child's filling. Each human body is part of the macrocosm. It is not just flesh and bones. What one person finds tasty maybe detested by another person. This is because, the constitution of each body is different and some tastes will not agree to one's body and hence they tend to avoid it. Here the focus is on taste and texture of the food. Fortunately in India, the ancient Siddha system of Medicine has thrown light on the body constitution and what kinds of food (depending mainly on their taste, texture etc.) are suitable for each body type. Here I have discussed a few major things that will help with the nutrition of kids:

1. To those kids preferring sweets and fried junk foods- use a lot of heating spices like cinnamon, cloves, bay leaf, turmeric, garam masala, and prefer cold pressed gingelly oil, groundnut oil, mustard oil over other oils. Such kids are advised to have regular heavy physical activity.

2. To kids preferring hot and spicy foods, eating more frequent meals in moderation – use same spices mentioned above in moderation, prefer fresh green chilli to dried red chilli or chilli flakes,

add freshly ground black pepper to recipes, avoid restaurant meals, avoid refrigerated foods, physical activity in moderation.

3. To those kids who sweat a lot, eating large meals, frequently passing stools, who become easily irritable, with a tendency to put on weight -include foods like Indian gooseberry, tender coconut water, use of coconut oil for recipes, lemon and avoid tamarind/chillies.

The above-mentioned points are only an approximate guidance and individual's food choices and preferences vary largely over the concerned individual and geographical location/time of the day/ mental and physical status etc. because the body constitution varies a lot and it cannot be generalized.

Most parents complain that they have a "fussy eater" when it comes to describing their child's dietary routine. It is difficult to make a separate meal for everyone in the house given the current work-life imbalance scenario. But what can be done is adding or subtracting a few spices here and there to make the food palatable to each palate because if we don't treat food as medicine then we might actually end up taking medications as food which will not be a pleasure at all.

"உணவே மருந்து".

It is imperative that the administrative bodies in each country revises the working hours of the population because it is humanly impossible to work for 8 hours, and then cook, clean, exercise, socialize, sleep in the remaining hours only to wake up next day to repeat the same cycle all over again. This lifestyle will kill many lives quicker than we can imagine. If only we had extra couple of hours, imagine how much each of us could accomplish and what gloriously meaningful lives we could live!

We are tempted to buy that readymade paratha with gravy or that frozen pizza while grocery shopping with the hope that it would give us some extra time to attend that party or go to that last minute scheduled meeting in a hustle. I can understand how difficult it is to chop veggies and make meals from scratch given the current hustling lifestyle. But even that can be made into a fun task everyday by involving the kids too in the meal preparation where they can contribute by chopping, cleaning, or doing the dishes. It is the chopping and washing the dishes that take a major chunk of the time of the entire cooking. It can be made as a fun family activity and it can provide a good time where you can bond with each other in the family, where you can ask your kid about their latest crush, or the thing that they did in school that day or just play some music and vibe together. It is these small things that matter. Not the expensive vacations that you plan once a year. Just buy an extra set of knives and cutting boards and you are all set to build a healthy loving close-knit family.

"Family that cooks together, Bonds Better".

Also, during these activities, you can easily pry into your kids' private lives and ask things that are of a little concern to you. Because during these tasks the analytical brain is focused on the chopping or whatever task that is given at hand, and the emotional brain has lost its guard. This is the time to know their deep secrets. These are the times when the conversation flows effortlessly and offence is not taken unless the questions are ridiculous in which case it may prove counter-productive.

Excretion

The fact that parents don't pay attention to their kids' bowel habits is specifically worrying to me. The brain is connected with the entire gut and hence each step in the process of digestion is intricately linked to the functioning of the entire brain. Many a times, the developing of a future anxiety or depressive illness can be prevented by treating the constipation that the person would have developed many days prior to the evolution of psychiatric symptoms. In a study that was conducted in my clinic in 150 patients who presented for the first time with anxious, depressive or psychotic symptoms, more than 87% of them had developed symptoms of constipation ranging from 7-14 days before the onset of psychiatric symptoms.

A person is supposed to have constipation if

1. They don't pass stools in the same time every day.
2. If they strain while passing stools or pass hard stools.

The parents are highly advised to tell their kids to inform them if they have constipation. If yes, please include a high fibre diet (locally sourced *கீரை வகைகள், நாட்டு காய்கறிகள்* are the best) and prefer locally grown vegetables and fruits. It doesn't make sense for someone in India to consume imported Dragon fruit for its vitamins and minerals. Constipation causes dysregulation in serotonin, acetylcholine and norepinephrine functioning in the brain, all the neurochemicals that are directly involved in manifesting mental illnesses.

Sleep

Sleep is necessary for the developing brain. A lot of changes happen during sleep. Benefits of a healthy sleep are:

1. The memories that are necessary for a productive life are stored forever, for example, the things that we read, skills that we learn etc. The emotion stirring events get deleted from the memory and are buffered in such a way that the brain does not react to that event/memory in a way that brings imbalance/suffering in life. This process is called "Consolidation" and it is done only during sleep.

2. Regulates equilibrium in all other areas of the body including the endocrine, reproductive, and gastro-intestinal system.

3. Reduces violent behaviour and aggression.

4. Regulates appetite and reduces unhealthy food craving and snacking.

5. Protective against life style diseases like diabetes, high blood pressure in the future.
6. Prevents depression and reduces the intensity of both physical and emotional pain experienced due to stress.

Children need to sleep longer than adults because the rapidly developing brain and body need more sleep to regulate the bodily functions.

An ideal sleep environment should be:

1. Devoid of noise and light.
2. Avoiding arguments or discussing conflicts before bedtime.
3. Having a good meal around 7-8 pm.
4. For some people having a glass of warm milk before going to bed helps.

We cannot compensate for under sleeping the previous night by over sleeping the next day. There is nothing called sleep debt. We incur long lasting changes in the brain by depriving it of sleep.

For example, we cannot redeem our sleep cycle by sleeping from 12 am – 8 am instead of 10 pm – 6 am. The quality of sleep from 10 pm – 6 am is entirely different from the sleep from 12 am – 8 am even though the duration of sleep remains the same.

It is always –

"*Quality over Quantity*".

However, once we become adults, our sleep cycle changes depending on our psyche (concept of mind), diet, physical activity, working style and pattern etc. which I have explained in detail in my book, "Buy Happiness from a Bookshelf".

<u>Dreams in children:</u> These are rudimentary and tend to involve everyday events. Some dreams are intensely emotionally charged and these need to be analysed in detail for therapy purposes. For example, a child who has a strict parent/teacher may dream of being chased by a lion. Here the lion is analogous to the strict parent/teacher and the helpless child expresses such anxious thoughts in dreams. Not all dreams are purported to have inner meaning. Being chased by a lion in a dream sometimes means just nothing.

Many of you who are living with kids would have experienced this – the kids become especially extra active just before bed time.

That is true. Unlike us, kids love their lives and hate to waste time by sleeping!

Healthy kids do tend to think that play time is the best time of their day. But it is essential for children (ages 5-11 years) to sleep around 9 pm and wake up around 7 am. It may tend to change by few minutes earlier or later in older children and teenagers. We must avoid encouraging the active thoughts and compelling stories that children bring up in the night time because if we pay attention and listen ardently, their stories are never going to end i.e., if we pay attention to their stories, they will continue talking and make up their stories with more enthusiasm and hence putting them to sleep will be difficult. This is how our behaviour shapes the children's behaviour.

Going to bed on an empty stomach is not advised as it may impair sleep and increase the risk of developing mental illness in the future in vulnerable individuals. Some kids have 3 square meals while some kids prefer 6-7 small meals. All this varies from individual to individual and this does not mean the child is fussy. Please do not force feed the children with the intention of promoting their health.

Primary School Children

The curse of the Indian child –

Many a time I am invited by schools to talk to school children with the purview of motivating them and to instill in them the importance of hard work and education. I wonder how the teachers and the school system hope to change the minds of hundreds of children by giving one small pep talk! This is not how we change a behaviour. In order to efficiently mold children to become a better fit for survival, we need to educate the parents, teachers and the politicians at large who make these ridiculous education policies including NEET exams.

This is the age where the bone cells are in full "vibe" and they need the right amount of food and physical activity to become stronger. This will not only impact their present life but play a vital role in postponing the onset of osteoporosis (a bone disorder where bones become fragile and break easily) in the future decades. It is a sad state to see the budding flowers strapped to their allocated benches in schools as if they are astronauts sitting in spaceships where even minor alteration from their assigned spots would signal a catastrophe.

At least 2 hours of unstructured group physical activity is advised for good physical and mental health.

Even for adults, they say "Sitting is the new Smoking". At this stage and age, we have come to the realization that we are certainly not so healthy as our grandparents and great grandparents were at our age. If we continue to live the same lifestyle, our children and future generations will become wheel chair bound sooner than we think.

What is unstructured group physical activity?

I want to take you back to the 90s when most of you were kids. Did we have a parent hovering over us all the time? Did we go to some class just for the sake of it?

When we played, we usually played with our neighborhood kids, random games and we devised our own rules for those games, and the rules evolved as our brains developed. Hence our brains were able to have more creativity, more ability to connect with even a stranger, more flexible when dealing with changing circumstances and compared to our kids, we were in a much better position to handle loss and suffering.

This is lacking in our kids' life because we are creating a life for them that is full of certainty and has immediate gratification.

It all starts when we hand a smart phone or an iPad to our kids so they eat without complaining. Eating is a pleasure in itself and has to be enjoyed each and every step of the process. When that process is distracted with a more passively stimulating electronic device, the brain is fully involved in consuming the video and it does not appraise or relish the food that is being consumed. In the initial years of growth when the body still has its innate intelligence, it is pertinent to bank on it, because when you like a certain food it is because your body needs that taste – this is a concept derived for the ancient SIDDHA system of medical sciences. Simply put, if you have a craving for a certain kind of food, this means your body needs that taste for functioning in equilibrium. For example, most children are fond of chocolates and ice-cream. This is partly due to the colourful and shiny packaging in which it comes. Looking at it from an eagle's viewpoint, the sweet taste in the above said food items reduces the vata and increases kapha. The kapha constitution is the one which favours the growth of strong bones and muscles. This does not mean that we have to feed chocolates and ice-creams to our kids, instead we will have to plan our kids' diet in such a way that kapha is naturally increased by including certain foods and spices in the diet. Kids crave the "sweet" taste in the chocolates and in the ice-creams. We can replace these food items with healthy home-made "sweets" like adhirasam, sweet seedai etc. by adding naatu sarkkarai and karuppatti vellam (நாட்டு சர்க்கரை, கருப்பட்டி வெல்லம்) instead of the usual white sugar.

Common problems noticed in kids aged 5-9 years

1. Not mingling with the rest of the class: Schools these days have a low student to teacher ratio (example: one teacher for 15 students, so there are only 15 students in a class). This may be

helpful for a child who has some special needs but for the other children this is a curse. You become richer by the number of different people you talk to. More the merrier. If there are a pool of 40-45 kids, then each kid has more probability of finding a friend who is compatible with him/her. Lesser the number of kids, lesser the chance of finding friends because they are just stuck with the definite set of 15 peers. Some kids may have interests other than cricket and cinema, so this kind of kid is going to find it difficult to conform with the others because the incidence of kids with interest in cricket is higher compared to the others; and in due course this kid may lose his/her unique potential and fall into the rat race just like everyone else. The concept of separating students based on their intelligence level at primary school should be strictly forbidden, because it is during such interactions the kids learn that each of them are unique and different and they need to look out for each other. This world is not full of people with an IQ of over 150. We fall within a broad range of abilities and we become humans only when we learn to co-exist in harmony with each other. It is these differences that make the world beautiful. Special children do need extra attention and it will help them cope better if they are surrounded by similar peers but to what extent? Not to the amount of warranting a special school for them. An extra classroom can be added to each existing school, where the regular kids can volunteer to teach, help them to eat, teach them to use the toilet etc. and such volunteering acts can be rewarded with the appropriate incentives so they understand that no good deed goes unreciprocated. For example, a kid who helps to take a child with special needs to the toilet, or a kid who teaches mathematics to another kid who keeps failing math consistently can be rewarded with a small amount of money or extra marks so they feel motivated to do so.

Let us see why some kids have trouble mingling with the others

(i) <u>Separation anxiety</u> – some kids find it difficult to cope up in an environment where there are no comfort figures in the vicinity (example parents/siblings etc.). This is quite common in kids and it usually wanes away with time. Some techniques like increasing the self-confidence of the child by instilling in him/her the reading spirit so that he/she spends more time studying and when they excel in the class, they enjoy the appreciation and the reward, and in due course the anxiety comes down.

(ii) <u>The shy introvert</u> – some kids just prefer being in their own space and are selective about who they share their energies with. For kids, this is not a conscious process but a subconscious one. This is not something to worry about. Depending on the situation, some kids tend to become more talkative while some maintain the same kind of communication style and it is perfectly fine to be so. Being an introvert may affect one's professional life, but the Facebook founder Mark Zuckerberg is an introvert!

(iii)   <u>Low intelligence (less IQ)</u> – In today's world, a person's intellectual ability is tested using a series of varied problem solving tests that give the result in the form of a number, higher the number – higher the intelligence. So if a child scores lower than the average on this kind of test, then he/she is said to have low IQ. Such children can be further classified as having mild/moderate/severe disability depending on their IQ scores. Children with mild and borderline intelligence levels may have trouble with communication and scholastic performance, but when given adequate consistent training they can be made to achieve independent functioning and living. If your child has trouble with communication, this is something we need to consider.

(iv)   <u>Autistic traits</u> – Some kids may have a delay in speech and find it difficult to relate to the other kids. This is suggestive of something called "autism" and it is not to dread of. People with autism have a different kind of brain where they are not able to understand the emotions of others and respond appropriately. This can be taught to them and they can be well functioning members of the society. Their brains are deficient in "Mirror Neurons" which are the basis of imitation learning (where we learn by observing others). Some kids with autism excel in areas like astronomy, neurophysiology, mathematics, playing chess etc.

(v) <u>Sign of depression</u> – not only among kids, even among adults depression can present itself as a tendency to isolate oneself, reduce communication with others etc. Unlike adults, children don't say that they are feeling sad because of something that happened, because the brain has not developed to an extent where they can make a connection between the way they feel and their thoughts and surroundings. This can be explored further by the class teacher who is the immediate contact of the child – talk to the child alone, make him/her comfortable, talk about the school activities, ask about the family members, etc.; as the conversation evolves the child will spill what's going on and then, with the consent of the child (sometimes consent is not needed), share the details with the parents and advise them to consult a psychiatrist as soon as possible. Because if a major depressive episode is not treated, then the brain loses some potential neurons that promote resilience which in turn will protect the mind from future emotional stressors.

The child must be taken to a psychiatrist even at the slightest suspicion of any underlying stress/difficulty.

(vi) <u>Underlying psychosis</u> – This is quite a rare occurrence but not impossible. Such kids may appear withdrawn and would not react as much to the happenings in the class. They need immediate psychiatric intervention.

(vii) <u>Abuse – physical/psychological</u> – Such kids should be handled with delicate care and if the parents are suspected of having a hand in glove with the abusers or if they are the abusers themselves then it should be promptly reported to the child protection services. However, in a country like India, this is debatable. Whenever we are dealing with children, the possibility of abuse should always be borne in mind. Usually, such perpetrators are someone familiar to the child and the child's family, example a relative or an uncle that visits often, less commonly the perpetrators can be a stranger too.

(viii) <u>Poor feeding/ lack of sleep/ urinary infections/ pain in the abdomen etc.</u> – are certain physical conditions where kids sink into their cocoon and hence must be thoroughly assessed should there be any change in behaviour.

Of all the behavioural problems, difficulties in socialization was mentioned first because the human brain has developed thus far because of its ability to communicate and co-ordinate with the others. If a child is deficient in getting along with the peers, then this heralds the origin of many more problems and psychological difficulties to come in the future. I really can't emphasise this enough. The ideal growing environment for kids should have healthy grown adults (preferably those who are not battling their own childhood trauma and displacing it on their kids), and other kids within 2-3 years as their age. This is the main reason we send kids to school, so they can learn to care, share, negotiate and pave their way to glory and independent existence.

Note to Teachers

I have not really had the best experience with teachers – neither as a student nor as a parent. It can be very demanding to deal with a whole bunch of kids, when they are all yelling and fighting at the same time.

1. As kids, it is their brain's early functioning coming into play where they learn:
    (i)   how to communicate,
    (ii) to select the tone that is needed for each conversation, and
    (iii) the amount of energy that is needed to attain a particular goal.

    The common tag line that teachers use is, "I need pin drop silence". I kindly request all the teachers reading this to please refrain from using this phrase. It is very cruel to stop the young brains from developing into masterminds in the future. The mantra here is "Talk, Talk, and Talk, just keep Talking". An hour a day must be drafted within the school time-table to allow for students just to talk to each other.

2. <u>Some kids are found to be talking excessively when being silent is absolutely warranted</u> – They create a ruckus in the class by talking all the time even when the teacher is taking class; climbing on tables and chairs when they are expected to sit and listen to what is being taught; inability to sit still; not paying attention when spoken to; losing and misplacing things constantly; failing to comply through a task, etc. are symptoms of a clinical condition called "attention deficit hyperactivity disorder" and there are many techniques and treatment strategies to manage this- don't break your head – this is not a problem worth breaking your head over, please consult a psychiatrist.

3. <u>The sad kid</u> – This warrants immediate attention. This kind of kid can be easily spotted when there is a joke shared in the class and all kids are merry making and laughing except for this child. This is a high alert situation and must be handled with care.

4. <u>The mature child</u> – These days it is not uncommon for primary school kids to behave like they are in their adolescence already. It may seem progressive but the most beautiful part of childhood is its

innocence and losing that may be the forerunner of many problems in the future. Imagine how happy you were when you thought the moon was secretly following you when you sat on the pillion of the bike while riding with your father? We should encourage children to experience childhood as much as possible because once lost, it can never be regained. If a developing brain is facing a traumatic situation it tends to mature faster in order to be able to cope up with the stress. This hastened process does not promote resilience but instead increases the vulnerability to developing anxiety, increases impulsivity, promotes emotional instability and depression in the adult years. Protective factors – treating the child like a child, avoid fighting with your spouse/parent in front of the child, give them a few small responsibilities but not large ones. Keep yourself genuinely happy because even if you don't say it out aloud, the kids will perceive the mental tension and angst in you and that may hurt them emotionally because more than wanting generous parents who buy them costly toys, they just want happy parents. Some parents try to make up for the lost time by showering their kids with expensive presents. Kids do not speak the language of money yet. They will love you if you simply play with them. Enter into their world, ask them what their latest interest is, talk in their language, create your own unique "Hello" and "Bye", as if it is a secret thing between you and your child; it is these kind of things that matter.

5. <u>The irritable/angry child</u> – A kid who keeps complaining all the time is someone who either has troubles at home/difficulty with homework or is constipated and is devoid of physical activity. If these needs are addressed, then they will become easier to get along with.

A 7-year-old child was brought to my clinic a few months ago because she refused to go to school and the parents were worried. I spoke to her and she was psychologically sound and intelligent, had no symptoms that could make her not want to go to school; then slowly she opened up saying that nobody in her class talks to her anymore. When I asked her why did she think nobody spoke to her, she replied, "I told the class teacher that my friend Pooja took my pencil and was not giving it back to me".

<u>Me:</u> Why was she not giving it back to you?

<u>Kid:</u> I don't know, I did not ask.

<u>Me:</u> Okay, so this is a problem between you and your friend, but why aren't the others not talking to you?

<u>Kid:</u> One day I complained about Leela (another classmate) to the class teacher, and then this Sathish (another classmate) was pulling my hair, so I told that also to the class teacher.

<u>Me:</u> Why did you tell all this to your class teacher?

<u>Kid:</u> Because my mother told me that if there is any problem with anyone in class, I should inform the class teacher.

In retrospect, this child does not have the capability to negotiate or to foster effective communication with a peer because here, the mother (whom the child believes is the most correct/just person in the world) had told her that she has to complain to the teacher if there is any disturbance in her equilibrium. Parents and teachers must be very careful about what advice and suggestions we are giving to our kids. They may seem mundane and insignificant to us but it may create an impact larger than we can imagine.

Here in this scenario, the child believes that there is always a teacher/mentor/elder person who will come to her rescue and protect her from all danger. But in reality, this is a ridiculous statement. It is important to instill a sense of safety in children's minds but they must also be taught bravery and the freedom to act out of their own free will to claim justice for themselves as long as it does not produce grievous hurt to self or others. As adults we know that all we have for us is ourselves and that no one is going to save us from danger lest be the danger. The essential element of independent living is not money, is not a job, is not owning a property, it is just having the guts.

"அச்சம் தவிர்".

Because of this, the other kids in the class have discriminated her and have started to avoid her. This social situation in some circumstances, may promote the brain's growth to develop symptoms of schizophrenia- which is a lifelong debilitating major mental illness.

If only this child had been motivated to negotiate, and deal with her problems then and there, she would not have refused to go to school and by now she would have had a fun gang of friends.

After few therapy sessions where her self-confidence and ice breaking skills were perfected, She was taught effective interpersonal communication skills, and now she goes to school happily.

6. <u>The violent kid</u> – This is by far commoner in boys than in girls. Parents are worried that he/she keeps hitting the others and always ends up in a local panchayat with the other kid and their parents. This can be easily managed in kids. In some children, when they are growing, a lot of inner tension is built and when the tension is not channelled properly the tension tends to come out as anger/diarrhoea/increased sweating. The ideal method to manage such anger outbursts is to enroll them in a Karate class. This may sound an oxymoron to some. Contrary to the popular belief, karate does not make a person violent. The different types of punches, kicks and the fight sequence(kata), all increase the *Parasympathetic* activity of the brain

and the nervous system. This activity is the one which promotes "calmness" in the brain and reduces the aggression. This means that with continued practice, kids will mellow down and become calmer and more amicable. This will also make them more compassionate and reduce impulsivity.

7. <u>Bullying</u> – Compared to the West, bullying is much less in India, but it is slowly picking up. Any act of bullying involves two kids with diametrically opposite character traits and tendencies: They are the perpetrator and the victim.

    (i) <u>Being the perpetrator</u> – Such kids are usually from broken families and troubled homes. They have a low self-esteem which they compensate by belittling the other kids through physical force and emotional torture. They enjoy the ego boost and attention they get by making fun of the other kids; the attention which the bullies have primarily not gotten from their homes/parents/ caretakers. When they hurt another kid, the bullies get a sense of accomplishment and an importance which makes them feel superior. Such kids need to be identified and the family members must also be included in therapy.

    (ii) <u>Being the victim</u> – Being a victim to such acts is certainly not the child's fault, but we will have to discuss the characteristics of such kids so we can eliminate the victim mentality and foster mental strength. These kids are usually the soft-spoken ones, they have poor academic performance, they don't excel much in sports as well. They are chosen as the victims because the bullies know for a fact that this victim will not talk back nor raise an issue. And just like the bullies predicted these victim kids suffer in silence. The only permanent solution for this problem is to encourage our children to be bold and talk back if their safety or dignity is threatened.

8. <u>Obedience vs Leadership</u> – This is a real-life incident that I witnessed both as a psychiatrist and as a karate teacher. He was an 8 years old kid. The parents brought him to consult me because they had gotten several complaints from his school teachers that he was being too mean to his peers in class and was always the loudest kid in the classroom. I spoke to him and soon realized that he does not have any underlying major mental illness. He had an average academic performance. From what the teachers had said, I understood he just had a few behavioural issues. On further exploration, he slowly opened up and said things like, "The boys are not obeying, they are breaking the rules, I am telling things for their own good, but they are not understanding". I suggested him to join in a karate class, to which he and his parents obliged.

And as I was also there in the same karate class, I had the chance to witness this child picking up all moves quickly, correcting other's postures and punches, always volunteering first for a Kumite (a fighting competition that is a part of Karate curriculum).

<u>Inference:</u> This is a child with profound leadership qualities, who finds it difficult to stand deviances from the expected state of perfection and he picks up fights with his peers when trying to correct them. The therapy for him would be to slowly impart the values of patience and empathy so that he gets to convey his point in the least offensive way possible. Once he masters that art, there is no turning back for him. He is sure to excel in any kind of group activity which he leads or any sport which includes team work (contrary to his initial presentation where his parents were worried that he was not getting along with his peers). This is how we try to understand a child despite all the accusations and make them live to their full potential.

It is not a compulsion that every kid must have a hidden talent and it is our duty to unearth it. Some kids do have special talents, while most of them don't. It is our duty to make kids self-reliant and ensure them a happy life, and not forcefully impart a highly competitive life that they are not willing to live.

Let them rather learn virtues like patience, empathy, kindness, loyalty, integrity.

Middle School Children

(Roughly between 10-13 years of age; this is only for a reference, the mentality of kids may largely cross over to higher or lower grades so there is no hard and fast rule).

The brains are still developing; especially around 11 years when the brain areas responsible for *Abstract Thinking* would develop. Abstract thinking is the ability to imagine and devise hypothetical plans and situations, come up with innovations and revolutionary theories. For example, the concept of "Facebook" is the brain-child of a visionary Mr. Mark Zuckerberg. Before he developed the code for this, he had an idea which did not exist in the then world. It was just an imagination in his mind, the imagination which changed the means of communication and networking. Roughly around 11 years of age, the brain attains a level of capability that can foresee ideas and make concepts out of thin air. With the current education system, where the kids are more likely to learn from rote memory by repetition, the abstract thinking may dwindle down to a trickle. As common people, we cannot challenge the education system that has metamorphosized into manufacturing memory buses for the factories. We can inculcate small habits like solving crossword puzzles, sudoku, even practicing kolams (கோலம்) (the practice in Tamilnadu where people draw patterns on the ground with rice flour), indulge them in reading a wide range of both fiction and non-fiction books, reduce screen time etc.

Reading

This habit alone can transform lives not only of the current generation but also of the future generations to come. The knowledge of the current affairs and history is represented in an extremely distorted manner in the school textbooks. I still wonder why kids in India should know about the World Wars I & II. The child's brain is more malleable and ductile compared to an adult's brain. Hence if reading is instigated in younger ages, it can benefit them in the years to come.

What books should they read?

All children should compulsorily be taught to read and write in their mother tongue or in a language that they largely communicate in at home. Language plays a vital role in the developing brain. Reading increases the vocabulary of the mind which in turn helps us articulate our thoughts and emotions better- which are the basics of survival. When we were hunter gatherers, we needed to be physically fit and brave enough to hunt the animals for survival. But, now in the 21st century, it is the words that we have at our disposal. If only this was taught in our schools, the Prime Ministers of countries wouldn't be waging wars with each other, instead of discussing the issues over a cup of tea and sorting it all out. When we are forced to learn a language that is not in vogue or necessary for our survival, the brain focusses all of its energy on memorizing the new language, lest use the resource for learning new information that might be useful for our survival. The Chinese, the Finnish, the Germans, the Russians etc. (the so called most developed and dangerous economies of the world), learn most of their school subjects in their mother tongue. No wonder the Finland has the most Ph.D. research scholars in the world. When we are taught to think in a different language, we run short of the words, lack capacity to understand the emotion behind the words, and its due meaning. This reduces our thinking capacity because we need a rich vocabulary to think and observe. For example, think of a flower. Now explain it to your friend or just think aloud to yourself: You certainly have a particular flower, the color, the tree, its location etc. This is what someone from a non-botany background can think of. If you are "into" Botany, you might have thought of the length of stamens and pistil, color of pollen, the scent exuded by the flower, carpels, sepals etc. We will have to know these words and the meanings of these words in order to imagine a flower in detail. Learning all these words is much easier in one's mother tongue and hence we need not spend hours memorizing jargon that would make only partial sense to us.

Let me use another abstract example: If you lost your money you would feel upset. Now try expressing this loss in your mother tongue and see how much more sense it makes in terms of emotion, content and context.

I don't intend to say Thamizh is the greatest of all languages, it may be, but to me personally I feel Thamizh is the only language/medium that touched portions of my heart that no man ever could! Figure out which language touches your heart and don't let go off that.

That being said, children's library should include books by authors from different socio-economic backgrounds, different countries, fiction, non-fiction, poetries, books on war, history, literature (preferably in their mother tongue), evolution, science, artificial intelligence, financial literacy etc. This is just a glimpse of the books that should be bought. Depending on the kids' interests the books can then be purchased under parental guidance and supervision.

Apart from this, some kids tend to show a specific liking and aptitude towards one form of art or curriculum. It is essential to identify such areas of strength and nurture them in that direction, so we don't waste the potential that already lies there in. For example, it is mundane to force a child to read a history book who clearly wants to pursue music and is excelling in it already. The teachers and the parents must liaise together and help draft a study plan for the child that will suit their personal interests and also help them to attain financial independence so they don't grow to regret their decision of choosing music over conventional education. Education was initially devised as a means to attain enlightenment by inner exploration. But now, the concept of education has transformed itself to something that serves as a means to get a stable job with a monthly salary. Money is essential for survival, and education is one of the safest means to attain it. What we fail to understand is even music is education. When you study music to become a musician, that music book is your curriculum. This is how we re-define education. Parents become worried when their child comes home one day and says, "I am going to pursue music". The uncertainty in this field is certain!

Hence a study plan must be devised by the child, parent and teacher in unison to come upon a plan that does not compromise much between following a passion and meeting the basic needs for survival.

In this age group, one hour per day must be allotted in school for kids to pursue different hobbies, read random books, if some are into sports then that can be encouraged. This is the age where the brain will benefit from structured classes. In this way, a sense of discipline is instilled in their minds so they learn that whatever they want never comes easy. Things that we get after a battle are always considered as prized possessions compared to one that we get with zero effort.

<u>For example, let us say your child asks for a toy.</u>

(i)   You buy it immediately.
(ii) You tell your kid that you will buy it for her/him if she/he gets above 70% in the exams.

Which among the two scenarios is more likely to witness the toy being handled with care and treated as precious?

You know the answer and why.

What is discipline?

This is a failed concept in the Indian system of education. People think discipline means getting up on time, brushing the teeth, wearing ironed uniforms, going to school on time etc.

Discipline means setting up a system of rules for the purpose of attaining a particular goal and following the rules until the goal is achieved. That is it.

If you want to run a marathon – you must eat right, do the regular exercises, sleep right etc.

If you want to become an IAS officer or a doctor – you must make it a habit to read and study every day, keep yourself physically and mentally fit, sleep right etc.

It is humanly impossibly for a child to get up and get ready wearing those ridiculous uniforms, going to school on time only to sit with the finger on the lips for 8 hours.

It is completely okay to take leave from schools for functions, for your grandparent's funeral, for your chithi/ chithapa wedding, for your cousins' kaadhu kuthu etc. There was a study conducted by a Harvard neuroscientist on what makes people happy and increases longevity. She found that the most important factor even before prioritizing physical and mental health was, having "meaningful relationships".

It is important for kids to know who their friends, family, relatives are and learn of their importance in life and to garner and maintain meaningful relationships with people whom they want to have in their life for a lifetime. They will never know whom to keep forever and whom to cut ties with, if we never introduce anybody to them.

It is quite common in some families to prevent their kids from talking to their cousins if they have a feud with their parents. Please end the generational trauma with yourself and don't pass it on to your children. Your enemies' kids need not be enemies to your kids. They can turn out to be best friends if only given the chance. If the kids themselves choose not to hang out with each other, then that is their choice. Also don't force kids of your best friends to hang out with your kids out of compulsion. Kids are also people with genuine emotions and likes and dislikes and that needs to be respected.

If that school gives a medal for 100% attendance then your child does not need that medal.

Obedience

If someone tells me, "Your child is very obedient", I will become really worried.

Some parents proudly proclaim, *"என் புள்ள இருக்கிற இடமே தெரியாது, அவ்ளோ அமைதியான பையன்"* – if this is how you describe your child, then please be informed that there are more chances for your child to be silently suffering from a mental health disturbance.

<u>Explanation</u>: For starters, children are naturally born to be inquisitive and have the need to explore the world around and to reason. The budding neurons (brain cells) are beginning to grow and branch out seeking out new synapses (connections). Each synapse stores a fact or more facts. Stronger the synapse, stronger the encoding of that lesson in the brain. For example, emotional memories have strong synapses, that is why it is difficult to move on quickly after a break-up. When the brain is not yet matured, it has an abundant potential to grow. A growing brain is identified neurobiologically by the increasing numbers of synapses. How will these synapses increase? – they increase by learning and reasoning.

How does the learning and reasoning increase? – this increases by asking questions. Yes, the more question a child asks, the more intelligent the child is going to be.

"What is this? Why should I do this? Who are you to tell me what to do and what not to do?" – these kinds of questions indicate the development of future scientists. So, if your child is one who keeps asking random questions, be happy

– your child may become one of the most intelligent minds of the future.

As parents and teachers, we usually expect the children to do as told. When they ask, "Why should I do this?", we are tempted to say,

"Because I said so".

The above statement burns the synapses because if the "Why" is answered a learning takes place, the synapse is formed, a lesson is learnt and then thereafter such consecutive learning promotes the formation of a strong foundation of synapses which will later help the child to score high in NEET exam!

But if the "Why" is not answered, then the enthusiasm and the hunger for knowledge dies away, synapse is not formed, the brain becomes one with low potential and this is the reason why most children perform averagely in schools and later go on to doing middle grade jobs rather than high paying jobs. They are also prone to becoming addicted to alcohol and other drugs in the future. The kids who usually excel in life (monetarily and based on level of subjective happiness) are the ones who never got their fire drained and were always curious about everything around and wanted to know why they had to do something instead of blindly obeying. This is important to build a strong nation because everything that we do needs to suit our current lifestyle and help us lead a happy meaningful life.

The "Why" kind of questions increase abstract thinking and when children are encouraged to think of alternative possibilities and provide better solutions, then they naturally become better at handling life and also in out-performing others in CAT and IITJEE exams because it is these kinds of problem-solving capabilities that are tested in such exams.

A child that never questions anything: This child needs extra stimulation and attention. It could be anxiety (most common), hearing or vision impairment, delayed brain development or a range of other disorders. Please do not look for a google diagnosis. Consult a psychiatrist.

Girls vs Boys

In most schools in Tamilnadu, there is a stigma about girls and boys sitting next to each other and in some schools, girls and boys are not even allowed to talk to each other because they fear that they might fall in love!

Please imagine this scenario – there are 5 plates in front of you. You can take any one plate you want with all of its contents. Worth of each plate is at least 1 million US dollars.

- One plate has diamonds,
- One has platinum jewellery,
- One has emerald stones (like the one Nita Ambani wore at her son's wedding),
- One has gold biscuits, and
- The fifth one is covered by a lid in a such a way that you cannot see what is inside it.

We already have all the precious and most expensive items in the first four plates. You can simply have 1 million US dollars by selecting any of the first four plates. Would the mind be okay with it or will it be curious to know what the fifth plate contains?

This is the inquisitive mind working. The covert (மறைவான) always attracts more attention than the overt (வெளிப்படையான). Likewise, when we deliberately discriminate girls from boys and strictly forbid them from talking to each other, the curiosity will increase and they will stop treating the other gender as equals and fail to understand that all beings have similar emotions. To such children the other gender will seem like an exotic species. This is the reason why many young girls fall trap to perverse unknown males because they are not able to identify the genuineness and the intentions of men from their speech. Men rape mainly because of a lack of empathy which would have developed had there been healthy interactions between girls and boys right from school life.

This is not only for the sake of safety but also on the professional front, men and women need to work together and be able to communicate better for comfortable peaceful working environment. Many kids, especially boys from government schools find it difficult to adapt to working environments where there are a lot of women because they were not allowed to mingle with them in their childhood. Most adults today have problems that stem from their childhood experiences. As adults it is our responsibility to create an environment where children grow happily and healthily (mentally and physically). We are reaping the benefits of the wars waged by thousands of our ancestors – be it freedom from slavery, right to education, right to vote, right to property, right to wear clothes and slippers etc. We did not do anything to be deserving of it, yet we are enjoying the harvest of the seeds sown by our ancestors. We are all just lucky to be born in this era where the plight of the common man is heard. We owe a lot to our ancestors and this debt can be repaid only by making it easier for the future generations. It is our birth duty to make it easier for the future generations.

These years (the age before a child enters teenage) are the last few years where the children's ability to obey and comply are at the maximum. Once they enter the teens, as the parental burden and worry increase so does the distance between them. I don't mean to discourage the parents, given the current living conditions it is imperial to understand the adolescent brain so we can learn how to deal with the rapidly developing neurons and burning synapses. This is important because in 10-15 years from now, today's kids are going to be the working force and they are going to be the ones ruling us! We better make them intelligent and disciplined so we don't get our own lives screwed.

The Teens

Let me start by taking a deep breath! As we have already seen, these are the last few years where the brain is maturing and the patterns we set at this point may last a lifelong. There are a few exceptions to this but not the norm. We shall study this by looking at a few problems which the kids presented with and analysis further on.

Hairstyles, hair colouring and character: It is during these years, the kids develop a sense of self, apart from the family they are born into.

The adolescent brain seeks answers to questions like –

Who am I?

Who are my people?

What do I like?

What I don't like? etc.

The answer seeking brain becomes quite strong. This is the time when the mothers will for the first time ever, get a sense of disgust from their kids' sweat. Until then, all parents would believe that their kid smells the best. That is the nature's way of telling us that until a certain age, kids need to be under our guidance and during adolescence, they are meant to grow apart from the parents. This is the way of life, the sooner we understand this – the better.

So, just into the pre-teen/teen era, the kids are programmed to develop a strong sense of self and are on the lookout for a peer group which they can identify with the most. Some kids who are more intellectually driven find peers who are on the same intellectual plane, share ideas and form a group. Some may take it a step ahead and wear matching bracelets/ colour the hair differently/ wear similar clothes/ use certain lingos/ etc.- all this differ from individual to individual. This becomes a problem when the parents and school administration pose stringent laws and restrictions on how a child should look. If kids learn that the way they look is something to be worried about and if they are judged for their external experiences, then this instills in them the idea that physical appearances matter. Like I had mentioned before, the more elusive something is, the more attractive it appears. So when a child is refrained from having a certain hairstyle or coloring it in a different colour, that particular aspect would mean a lot to them and they would focus all their energy on procuring it. I never understood the logic behind many school teachers hiring barbers to cut the school children's hair short.

I questioned the teachers why they did so and all of them said, "He doesn't look a school kid. He looks like a porikki (rogue in Thamizh)".

Then I asked them, "If a kid has his hair cut short and has viboothi in his forehead, how does he look like?". They had no answer.

This concept of labelling a kid as "porikki" just because he is poor and has a certain hair cut is rooted deeply in Sanatana dharma. This thought process should change and teachers should stop focusing on meagre things and focus on things that really matter.

The reason why kids tend to have the so called "extreme choices" is because they are figuring who they are and what they want. This is the age that is exactly meant to answer those questions. As long as it does not hurt the self or the others, any habit can be encouraged. As time passes, the kids will soon realise what they want and choose depending on their likes and dislikes. If we don't even give a chance to these kids to experiment (not talking about recreational drugs/ abuse), they will have absolutely no idea whatsoever and will eventually end up living a life that is expected of them and not what they want to do. This will result in another generation of grumpy old adults unsatisfied with their work and life.

Also, if adults keep pressurizing them on these mundane things, they will lose respect for us because according to them, "We are always telling them don't do this/ don't do that". Our words will be respected only when said once in a while, not when we keep correcting them every now and then, in which case we will be seen as "nagging".

Have you ever thought why people get addicted to gambling?

We all know gambling is dangerous. 85% of the first-time gamblers say that they started gambling knowing very well the dangers of it and they were very sure that they would not gamble after they lost a certain amount of money. Yet they got addicted to it. How?

When you gamble, you have no idea whether you will win or lose. It can be a win or you can lose. The result is unpredictable. And we never know how many losses we have to take to win once. This is called – variable ratio/ variable interval type of reinforcement.

<u>Variable ratio</u> – There is no guarantee that losing 10 times must give a win the eleventh time. You can win the second time or at the 100th time or never!

<u>Variable interval</u> – There is again no guarantee that you will win after one hour of playing or after 12 hours of playing. You can even win the next second.

This is a type of learning that produces the strongest connections in the synapses, because the thrill of not knowing when we are going to win, makes us gamble more and more. "Just one more time" is the motivation behind the strong addiciton to gambling.

In this context, our children are going to make umpteen mistakes all their lives. If we keep correcting each and every mistake (this means losing every gamble), the learning is not well established because the kids get bored and lose value for our words.

Instead, if we correct only the major mistakes (which will be a lot less) the kids will learn that the parents/teachers are not unreasonable and may actually think that they might have a point.

On a lighter note: It is after all just hair! It is going to grow back, once cut. It is not a life or death issue. Let them enjoy little of the hair they still got because adulthood has a whole other range of problems including hair fall!

Children, Violence and Terrorism

During adolescence, as I have mentioned before, the brain and mind seek a sense of identity and belongingness. Some kids find a purpose that adds to their social and economic metric while some do things that are counter- productive.

Violence

We resort to physical violence (behaviour involving physical force intended to physically hurt, damage, or kill someone or something) when we are unable to communicate the emotions that arise from within through words and when we are unable to get the intended outcome from the people whom we are having a conversation with. The reason for this is the lack of adequate vocabulary to name the emotions and an inability to regulate emotions. Exercise or involvement in sports and reading can largely help to reduce the violent aggression in children and adults

In India, Terrorism is defined as, "An act that threatens the unity, integrity, security, or sovereignty of India, or that intends to strike terror in the people of India or a foreign country". In other words any action or idea that is against the governing body.

If you take the case of any so called "Terrorist", they/he/she has/have a very strong sense of identity and purpose. These are people who have been recruited into their teams from a very young age, coerced into believing their collective purpose and are trained meticulously to attain a particular goal. When we talk about terrorists from the Indian perspective, all of us will be aware of the strained political scenario along the Jammu Kashmir border. The joy most Indians get when the Pakistani cricket team is defeated by the Indian cricket team in the World Cup is immaculate. There are strained political connections that form the root of this problem. The conflict is between two Prime Ministers who cannot sort out this issue by having a decent conversation and finding a common ground where each party can be benefitted without disappointing the other in a critical way. Instead they chose to recruit the young fit India/or (any other country for that matter) to fight at the border and lose their precious lives over an imaginary geo-political boundary.

<u>The reason adolescents are recruited is because:</u>

    (i)   They are more gullible.

    (ii)   Their thirst for a sense of belonging is quenched by the soul stirring histories and stories that they are taught by the so called "terrorist" groups.

(iii)   In the setting of emotional distrust within their families and current social ties, a group that appears to be warm and accepting them of all their flaws is appealing to the young minds and they feel safe and secure within that group.

(iv)   A new identity for the self is formed and this identity is not confined to social ties and a sense of liberation is reached. They are given an identity that is larger than humanity and believe that they are working for a higher purpose and are selected by a higher entity to fulfil certain responsibilities.

(v)   The joy and liberation that follows is limitless and they continue following the same principles taught to them by the so called "terrorist" groups.

(vi)   Once they develop trust and become loyal followers to their leaders, they are assigned small tasks to complete and are rewarded heavily on completion. This rewarding behaviour surges the dopamine level in the brain especially for those kids who have been chronic misfits in their society.

(vii)   Soon, they are introduced to firearms and introduction into their own military starts.

(viii)   In the modern day, firearms have been replaced by AI. In this scenario modern day hackers are targeted and recruited to gain access into the country's mainstream defence and data agencies.

(ix)   A bunch of adolescents with no sense of purpose or responsibility are a threat to the society. They have to be identified, properly guided to attain self sustainability.

Effects of short and long term stress on the immune system

Most people believe that children who are exposed to difficult life circumstances will grow up to become "strong" people. I strictly forbid the use of the word "strong" when talking about mental health. This will imply that if someone buckles under pressure then they are all supposedly "weak". Strength and weakness here are not individual's choice but their ability to face adversities. So if we label a person as "weak" then this becomes "blaming the victim" mentality where we shift the illness cause from neurobiological fallacies to attitude fallacies. This means a person's ability to deal with hardships and brave through difficulties depends largely on the biochemical make-up of the individual's body and much less on the so called "attitude" that most people ascribe to, "It's all in your head, just snap out of it".

Studies show that short term stress – (perceived difficulty of any kind, lasting for a short duration (hours to weeks) and culminates in a desirable life outcome) makes the individual more resilient because the brain learns that no matter what the difficulty, there is always light at the end of the tunnel. This creates brain connections that fire up in terms of adversity but because there is hope (which was learned through past life experiences where a short term stress was relieved by a desirable outcome) the brain stops producing stress hormones after a short span because the brain has learnt that the stress will wane away after a while and hence there is no need for the brain (hypothalamus) to produce enormous amounts of stress hormones and so the brain easily copes up and starts secreting more *serotonin* (the happiness hormone) anticipating future happiness. The immune system in turn is upregulated by the fluctuating *cortisol* (stress hormone) secretion and there is a surge of anti-inflammatory cytokine release that helps to deal with the current and future stress and this builds up resilience, making the individual "strong". For an additional point here, there are certain foods that are high in a chemical called, "**Anthocyanin**" which help improve immunity – example karuppu kavuni rice (கருப்பு கவுனி அரிசி), red rice, blueberries, red banana (செவ்வாழை), red onions, pomegranates, brinjal etc.

In unfortunate situations when an individual is exposed to long term stress (months to years) or chronic mental illness, the stress response triggered by the brain goes unchecked and there is surge in cortisol which in turns alters the functioning of the entire body. Here the levels of cortisol and inflammatory markers are high because the body/mind/brain has never seen the light of day and are lost in despair because their current stressful life situation seems to be never ending and there is no hope for the future. Given this circumstance, the immune system is disrupted, secretions of serotonin is decreased at large and the brain becomes "weak". This leads to the individual succumbing under the slightest pressure and losing it all!

It is just a wonderful stroke of luck for most people who have never had to experience long term stress!

We have read a lot about long term and short term stress. What is stress? Some say poverty is stressful, some say broken families are stressful.

The widespread belief is that poverty is stressful.

Why?

Material poverty (வறுமை) is the only stress that can be quantified easily and visualised by the naked eye. Stresses like the struggle of a mental illness or an absent father is not measurable. So the latter becomes "an attitude problem". Most people see kids who are mentally ill from well to do backgrounds as "the rich spoilt brat" and criminally refuse to acknowledge the suffering and distress that the child undergoes. This will lead on to many problems and difficulties in the futures of both the child and that of the entire nation at large.

There is no universal definition of stress. What one person perceives as stress maybe a blessing for another. For example: the burdened Indian housewife may dream of owning a company and becoming a CEO, whereas the CEO may dream of having a family. It is entirely subjective.

But for the sake of understanding, an individual can be said to be stressful when:

(i)   They are obligated to do something they "CANNOT" do. Here it means an inability to perform a certain a task. They may be poorly equipped, experience a lack of understanding of the facts that is required or a lack of efficient means to complete a task etc.

(ii) They are obligated to do something they "DON'T WANT" to do. Here it means a lack of like or desirability to do something. For example, being stuck in a job that you don't like.

Therefore we can never predict with certainty what a stressful situation is. It is requested to readers to be kind to everyone you meet because you have absolutely no idea the amount of stress a kid/an individual / an adult is going through to make it to school/office that day. Some so called "intellectuals" debate that no matter what the situation is, how you react to it determines the level of stress. Please stay away from people with such baseless concepts and theories because nobody would ever consciously choose "suffering" from a range of emotions.

<u>If a child is presented with emotions on different plates</u> – like

1.   Joy
2.   Happiness
3.   Euphoria
4.   Frustration
5.   Disappointment

6. Excitement
7. Suffering

Do you think that anybody would ever choose options 4, 5 or 7?

NO.

"கனிஇருப்பக் காய்கவர்ந் தற்று".

Nobody chooses to suffer. Suffering is an inevitable (*தவிர்க்க முடியாத*) choice of an unfortunate mind.

The best you can do is be kind and non-judgemental. Take the child to a psychiatrist at the earliest.

The 10th and 12th board exams

The drama surrounding these exams are the most useless in the whole of the world. The modern school system lasting for 12 years was introduced no earlier than the second half of the 18th century. Until then, only a particular sector of the society had access to education and even among them learning and education was considered as a lifelong process and not confined to a set of years. Even before that, (I am talking about more than 10,000 years ago) there were scientists whom we now call as **"Siddhar"** (*சித்தர்*) who had tremendous expertise in various fields of science, medicine and astronomy. Their knowledge on plants has not yet been deciphered completely even today owing to their complexity and brevity. This is interesting because not any random person can become a siddhar. In order to be considered an expert in a certain field, the interested individual has to present the data and findings in a forum full of senior "siddhar" and mentors and guides, all of whom will debate upon the presentation and then can either accept or reject it. This is akin to the present day conferences and peer-reviewed journals. If only more funding is invested in reviving the ancient siddha science, maybe we can cure diabetes and hypertension and also a range of mental illnesses! This has been my dream for quite a while now and I hope this dream sees the wake of dawn one day.

<u>Coming to school education:</u> 10th and 12th:- these exams were designed to filter the high achieving students so that they can be admitted to colleges based on the marks and ranks they scored in these exams. This has largely narrowed down the potential of students because when the complete focus lies solely on the 12th Board exam marks, the marks of 10th Board exam become obsolete. Some parents are panicking over the academic prowess of their kids in 10th Board exam because if the marks come down, then they may not be able to get the desired group in higher secondary school, (the most competitive group in higher secondary as on date appears to be the first group where both mathematics and biology are taught). The wide consensus is that if their child enrols in this group, there is an option of opting for both Medicine or Engineering in college.

The first panic

Low marks in 10th may not get them into the first group.

1. This holds true only if they are planning to send the kid to the same school. There are hundreds of thousands of schools in Tamilnadu which are densely located where you can never run short of schools to send your kid to.

2. If your kid is not able to get into the first group in the same school, then please find another school which will be happy to accommodate any new kid.

3. Indian parents still see it as their "status" to send their kids to a certain school. This mentality should change. Your social status will depend on how you treat others and not on which school your kids go to.

The many panics before the first panic

When the school curriculum is set up in a way where the maximum/only importance is given to the 10th and 12th marks, the scores obtained in the preceding years make no sense.

1. Nobody is really going to bother if your kid does not know the year in which Mahatma Gandhi went to Dandi march.

2. If this curriculum is changed, then more concentration can be given to methods that foster independent thinking, problem solving, how to make friends, how to deal with setbacks, failures and break-ups, rather than making kids memorise random facts that are not going to be of any use.

3. Instead of assessing students potential through written exams, the exam pattern can be changed to multiple choice question types, so they will try to understand concepts instead of memorising volumes and volumes of books. The question paper pattern can be changed where a major chunk is given to one word answers and a small percentage is devoted to essay type answers.

4. The school curriculum is the one that has not been updated since many years. A thorough cleanse must be given to the school textbooks and the education can be given in a way which makes the kids feel, "I am really grateful I studied and learnt all this in school".

5. Many schools assign "nonsensical" work in the name of projects which are eventually done by the parents or a smart business owner who has understood the weakness of parents who would spend an arm and a leg to make their kids get that "A" grade. Instead, this can be catered to certain kids who are interested in arts and crafts and they can be encouraged to pursue this as a subject, while the others can find something else to learn or simply enjoy the time playing with friends.

6. Many subjects must be made available in schools as electives to be selected from the 6th grade so they can gain more knowledge in specific fields and can become experts soon. For example, few

kids who are definite about becoming doctors, can be made to spend a major chunk of their time on biology and a lot less time on math.

7. Artificial intelligence is going to take away most of our jobs and that in turn will create new jobs that requires experts on coding and artificial intelligence. The kids need not wait until college to learn the basics. Classes on artificial intelligence must be started from 6th grade while the World Wars can be saved for kids who are specially interested in War History.

The second panic

Neither parents nor kids sleep peacefully during the whole of the "12th" standard.

What are these 12th standard marks used for?

1. To get into a good engineering college.
2. Nothing else.

Now with the introduction of NEET exam for admissions into medical colleges, the 12th final Board exam marks are not a must.

For all other courses, the competition is not as high as that for engineering and hence exceptionally high marks are not warranted.

At the end of the day what matters is – coming to a realisation that nothing in life is worth losing your peace and happiness.

In India, parents usually infuse the idea that their kids owe them something in return for providing them with food and shelter. When you tell your child, "You have to think of the sufferings your parents went through. You have to study for us, do you know how much your father is sacrificing so you could go to a good school?", – this instils in them a strong sense of guilt (which is the forerunner of developing major depressive disorder) when they fail to meet your standards of expectation. Also as I have said before, your kids don't owe you a single damn thing. If you and your spouse feel that you are suffering to meet ends and sending your child to the most expensive school, then it is your fault to have even decided to have a child in the first place where you cannot give your child the bare minimum. You are obligated to give your child the basic needs for survival.

The thought that we need to give to the children is, "You have to study for your own survival. If you study, you can probably get a decent paying job and then that will help you live without suffering. Your life is partly your responsibility". Parents fail to give their kids a minimum sense of responsibility and this makes them dependent on an adult for all petty issues which will eventually lead to the building of a nation with adult babies who are incapable of taking care of themselves.

It is also important to not make kids take complete responsibility for everything that happens to them.

We see all motivational speakers screaming, "If you want it, you can achieve it. Follow your dreams. Everything is possible. If he can, then you too can".

The harsh reality is not everything happens to everyone. Certain things just don't happen no matter how much we try. We will have to build the temperament which says, "I will be okay even if it doesn't happen".

Among people who pursue fine arts as a profession, the majority of them come from a wealthy background.

<u>This implies:</u>

1. Fine arts don't pay well.
2. In order to pursue music or painting as a career, you have to have rich parents.
3. Even if you want to major in Art, first make sure you are able to stand on your own feet and then you can run.

As glamourous as it may seem to pursue one's dreams, it is quite a gamble to risk it all at the possibility of an unguaranteed outcome. Whoever you are, whatever your social status is – the first step in pursuing a career must involve planning a source of income which could keep you afloat. Once your life is stabilised, then all the glitz and glamour can be pursued. This is a wiser way of planning a life and career rather than jumping head on into a non-promising venture.

To make this more clear:- thousands of students are enrolled in various doctor producing factories (NEET coaching schools) but only few are able to crack it. I don't mean to discourage individual effort or undermine a student's capabilities, I am trying to point out that it is detrimental to make students believe that they are the sole reason for their failure. In such circumstances, students internalise these failures and believe *"I am a failure"*, instead of thinking *"I have faced a failure"*. This is why we have to detach them from taking internal responsibility to a certain extent but not completely.

The outcome of having a strong sense of right and wrong

He is a 15 year old boy studying in tenth standard. His parents are very strict in upbringing kids and right from a young age, he was taught in depth about what is right and what is wrong. His mind has developed to observe the world through a black and white lens. This means he fails to see shades of grey. As humans we are all fallible and we can never be either all right or wrong at all times. Each individual has his/her unique thought patterns and likes and dislikes and hence all beings cannot be grouped into one particular well defined model.

In his curriculum, he has studied about female genital organs and when he and his friends had a discussion about the female reproductive parts, he was completely grossed by that and felt disgusted as he was told by his parents that talking about sex or genitalia is "**Wrong**". When this happened, his entire mind was filled with a particular word representing the female reproductive part. This boy who had a conservative and orthodox upbringing was not able to handle the conflict in his mind which arose because -

1. His hard wired brain was taught that "sex" was wrong.
2. Now owing to his adolescence where talking about sex was the norm of human evolution process, his rigidly moulded brain was unable to accept the fact that he had to study and write about this for the purposes of his exam.

Because of this internal conflict – (where his old learnings told him to avoid even thinking about it and his current life demanding him to learn about it), he developed severe distress and the word "vagina" kept flashing in his mind over and over again and he was not able to control it. The distress can be understood only by people who go through it or by trained professionals who treat it. I have seen many parents tell me that, "He is imagining it all unnecessarily". Families and friends never seem to understand the suffering of such kids and they just brush it aside saying, "It's all in his head".

"அவனா கற்பனை செஞ்சிக்கிறான்" – when people say this, they are subconsciously undermining the suffering of the patient and blaming him for his illness.

People don't understand that this is a disease because they lack the awareness of such mental health issues and more importantly such suffering cannot be seen by the naked eye like a wounded arm or a leg. Such knowledge must be shared with the general population.

Not all kids brought up with strict sense of morals, grow up to develop mental health issues. Only some kids have troubles like this and it is not their fault. Some brains have a tendency to develop mental health issues which is mostly genetically determined, and it is these brains that must be given more attention by providing healthy stimulating environments to grow and flourish. They buckle even under minor stressful events.

Another important reason for the increase in the development of mental health issues these days is the continued practice of marrying within the same caste (ஒரே சாதி திருமணங்கள்).

For example, there is an enzyme called "pseudo cholinesterase" in the blood which is deficient in a community of people called the "naatu kottai chettiar" (நாட்டு கொட்டை செட்டியார்). This enzyme is used to metabolise the medicine given for anaesthetic purpose so that the patients don't feel pain while undergoing surgery. When people from that community are operated under anaesthesia, they never recover from the anaesthetic affect. This means they will never be able to wake up after the surgery because they don't have this special enzyme that ends the action of the anaesthetic medicine. So, all anaesthetists ask this question, "What is your caste?" to their patients so they can administer another special drug that does not need the above said enzyme.

The biological reason for this is – due to repeatedly marrying within the same caste, the genes (because they are all the same gene expressing themselves over and over again through successive generations) lose their strength and all the weak genes are expressed leading to production of weak children. When you see the population at large, in Tamilnadu especially, the average height of the population has been decreasing and breeding within the same castes and families have been found out to be one of the main reasons.

When we think about mental health issues, all psychiatrists ask patients what religion they follow to understand their belief systems and the philosophy of the self. So far we have not been educated to ask the caste of the patient. But if the "Same Caste" marriages continue then more diseases (mental and physical health issues) will be classical of certain communities and we will be faced with the woeful situation where psychiatrists and other doctors are forced to ask the community of the patient to help them diagnose certain disorders and clinical conditions.

How the problem in this boy could have been prevented?

In parenting, while it is critical to teach them what is right and wrong, it is also essential to give a leeway for shades of grey/for certain issues where there cannot be stringent classification of right and wrong. Children need to be taught that being right and wrong doesn't always matter and what matters is how kind and understanding we are of others.

The importance of exercise is highly under estimated. Regular exercises or involvement in any sports activity must be encouraged.

A diet high in fibre and protein must be advised while refraining from refined ultra processed foods.

Downsides of junk food:

These foods are craved by children especially adolescents. The common reasons are:

1. <u>Boredom</u> – The teenage years are meant for growth, exploration and developing a passion. When such stimulating environments are not provided, the brain falls short of dopamine and eating becomes an easy coping mechanism to combat the deficient dopamine. Keep them occupied and they will happily eat whatever you feed them.

2. The adolescence is the growing stage where metabolism is high which leads to rapid decline in glucose. Hence snacking seems to be an effective means to keep up the glucose levels. This problem can be averted by replacing polished white rice

with low glycaemic foods like traditional varieties of rice, millets and including locally grown fruits and vegetables.

3. <u>The crispy nature of the packed foods</u> – evolutionarily we have grown to be attracted to crispy/crunchy fruits and vegetables, because while we were foraging hunter gatherers we were starved of nutrition for most days and when we stumbled upon a crispy apple or crunchy vegetable (this means it is a fresh produce), we ate it with vigor with the hope it will keep us satiated for the next few hours or days. This brain (more akin to the animal brain) is still inside all of us. The evolutionarily ultra refined complex problem solving new brain that we have now is fully functional only at a time of both physical and mental wellness. During adolescence if we do not take proactive effort to nurture the intellect, then the kids will certainly regress to the early man's brain and crave junk which has replaced the olden day crunchiness of fresh fruits.

4. <u>The MSG poison</u> – the chemical glutamate is naturally found in breast milk. Another version of it called – the monosodium glutamate is a chemical that is added to all processed foods with the view of making it tastier and create craving in our minds. This is the reason why everyone gets easily addicted to junk foods irrespective of age and gender.

The idea of a perfect family:

She is studying in her first year of college at a different state in India. 18 years at home and this was her first experience staying away from home. It was a different culture, different language, entirely a new world. She initially struggled but a few weeks down the lane, she learnt to cope up and was faring well in her exams and maintained good inter personal relationships with her peers. She spoke to her parents and siblings over the phone and was well connected to her roots. She and her gang of 4 other students made good friendship with each other and provided safe environment to be their true authentic selves. She had nothing to complain about. Her life was "perfect". But as we all know, there is no life that is "perfect".

A few weeks ago she came to know that her father whom she had always looked up at, has been having an extra marital affair. He also has kids in that relationship. Her world shook. She was not able to digest this. Her idea of perfect family and world came crumbling to the floor. She began skipping her classes, lying in her bed all day ruminating about her past. All the excuses that her father made to her for his absences during festival times seemed to make more sense to her now. She had 3 step siblings about whom she had no idea whatsoever. She felt deeply responsible for her younger brother whose world has been equally shattered. Her younger sister was coping up well and she had started to take things in her stride but SHE was still upset and felt betrayed. Soon this feeling pervaded into all her other areas of life – she stopped hanging out with her gang, isolated herself, did not go to the hostel mess for food, starved herself as she did not feel like eating, refused to bathe even after pressing by her roommates owing to her stench. She became miserable. As she was an intelligent student fortunately, she did not fall prey to the "drug" seeking culture that prevailed in her campus.

The salient feature to be discussed here is:-

Why she was not able to handle this while her sister was able to completely overcome this even though both of them were brought up with the same values, had the same parents, ate the same food and went to the same school?

1. Even though we all see the same movie, each of us have different perspectives about it. We all LOOK at the same things, but SEE them differently. A study was done on the kids of parents who were addicted to alcohol and other drugs. There were marked differences in the character traits of even identical twins who witnessed the same father and grew up in the same household. 65% of the identical twins went on to develop the same addiction that their fathers had, while the remaining 35% of them strictly forbade themselves and all their friends from considering drinking alcohol even for recreational purposes.

2. We can never predict or conclude how a person should or should not behave under any circumstances for we have no idea what they

are SEEING as opposed to what everyone is LOOKING at.

"பார்வையை செலுத்தும் இடம் வேறு,
பார்ப்பது வேறு".

We all may look at a rose, but see differently. For example, when I *look* at a rose I may *see* "love", when my sister *looks* at a rose, she may *see* a "flower", when my mother *looks* at a rose, she may *see* "her mother who passed away".

A lot of distress and suffering was felt by the patient in this "perfect life" scenario because of the difference in her mind between what she "saw" and what actually happened. The life that happens to you is simply a story that you keep telling yourself.

When the equally addicted kids of alcohol addicted parents were asked -

Why did you start drinking? – they said – "Because I have seen my father drink".

When the sober/teetotaller kids of the same alcohol addicted parents were asked -

Why did you NOT drink? – they said – "Because I have seen my father drink".

If we let go off the idea in our thinking style of how it is all supposed to be, life becomes a little easier to live.

Following few weeks of therapy and some medications, she made a beautiful recovery.

And she said, "My life is perfect again....................."
She paused. "............... It will be no matter what happens!"

This is what I mean by beautiful recovery. Changing the cognitive structure of a child can pave way for more green pastures in their lives.

Why is everyone concerned about being "perfect" or having "perfection"?

Social media plays a large role in garnering a sense of "lack" in everybody's lives. These days everything is a celebration with glitz and glam. What was once under the sole proprietorship of the rich and famous has now become the norm of the majority. It is not a sin to find a reason to celebrate, for life is all about finding random reasons to celebrate and create joy. Now it has become mandatory to celebrate every life event and showcase it to the whole world. This phenomena has caught up in the last decade and is gaining momentum. The reality of this can be explained by analysing the concept of posting the kids' achievements online including on WhatsApp, Facebook, Instagram etc.

Parents find abundant joy in showcasing to the world their kids' first steps, the moment when they crawled over, the medals they got for reciting a poem by heart, the prize for securing the first mark in each grade etc. It is natural for every parent to get excited over the achievements of their offsprings. This soon becomes a toxic culture where every parent has a covert need and desire to compete with the other parent. Kids are oblivious to these initially but soon they catch up through the process of "learning and modelling". This means that children learn quicker through observing the behaviour of their parents and friends than through preaching or disciplining. The competence behaviour if left unchecked progresses to venomosity and creates a sense of unrest where winning becomes the goal. The need to be first is desirable but not at the cost of focusing narrowly on the outcome without enjoying the process. When the goal becomes the solitary metric, then life becomes a series of chasing goals one after the other without even having the ability to enjoy the fruits of victory.

Whatever personal life updates we see on WhatsApp statuses and Instagram stories are only a highlight reel. People are not going to be sharing pictures of the nights they cried themselves to bed or the times when they had a bad fight with their spouse. We tend to extrapolate the joyous moments of others to their everyday life and think that everyone else is leading a happy successful life while dwelling on the thought "Only my life sucks, why am I suffering?" This results in a subconscious bias that one-self is given a bad life while the others are bestowed a gifted life with choicest blessings. What was once a private issue in life is now becoming a topic of discussion in family, friends and even on office WhatsApp groups. On the contrary, social media is playing a religious role in increasing the numbers of friends while reducing the quality of the friendships. For example, on your birthday you may get thousands of wishes from everyone on the various WhatsApp groups you are in; how many of the wishes are really wishes from the heart? Would you rather have someone call you and wish you or just send you a text message? It is only a few select members of friends and family groups who matter and who actually care. We should not lose them in the pursuit of chasing everyone.

Once we come to the realization of AI and the notorious effects of social media in our lives, we should encourage our children to foster genuine relationships with the "offline people". Kids no longer speak to the kids sitting next to them. They are happily chatting with a friend who is in a different area whom they believe to be the one person who "gets them". They believe that it is that one particular long distant friend who would understand their feelings and emotions. When we put this thought into analysis – they are emotionally close because they are physically distant i.e., if they get to spend each and every second of their life together, living in the same house and sharing everyday emotions, those kids would grow to hate each other. When in distance, they don't perceive each other's every miniscule change in emotion which the parents perceive. This is the reason why teens consider the adults as their enemies and the adults can't stand them either.

What they are speaking over the phone to their friend is just sharing a story from their own "one-side" and their friend has no idea about what exactly happened because they have not heard the other side of the story. This is another reason why our kids' friends hate us equally.

The social media has now become a measure of our developmental milestone as an adult. This measure is of no use to anybody and we should take conscious efforts to avoid being influenced by the brilliant flawless portrayal of other's lives and strive to live a fulfilling life ourselves.

The Indian Mother

In the western countries gender is never a topic of discussion or debate when it comes to parenting and running the household. All the old and some new Indian dads believe that gender is a social construct where the female of the species is "obligated" and "supposed" to cater to the needs of the spouse, the children and the in-laws. Most men prefer "working women" as wives. But once married, they expect the woman to jeopardise her career, take care of him and his family including the extended family members, cook, clean, find a new job in his locality, and go to that job while tending to all the before said chores. The Indian mother is one resolute multi-tasker. Even science has refuted that the concept of multi-tasking no longer exists. When people manage to get various tasks done, they are actually "task switching" and not multi-tasking. But when you observe the Indian mother- all theories of science, time and stamina come to a standstill. She runs on horse-power unit of energy and consumes water as fuel. The common working Indian mom alias the "super woman" wakes up earlier than the rest of the family, makes morning tea, breakfast and lunch, gets her kids ready for school, goes to work, comes back from work, does all the dishes (sometimes maids are employed to aid in this), makes dinner, calls her parents and ensures their well-being, completes her responsibilities for the day and then goes to bed.

I need not explain in detail the life of most of the working Indian male. It is out in the open for everyone to see.

He just goes to work and takes food on time.

It is surprising to see a few progressive men becoming ideal husbands where they share every household chore and children of such parents grow up to become the real pillars of the nation.

The difficulties faced by the Indian mother and its impacts:

She toils and toils until one day when she can take it no more. That is the day she is brought to seek professional help because if she is sick there is no other person to run the house. Hence, she is expected to make a quick recovery and resume her duties as soon as possible. On further exploration she expresses her need of carrying the burden of the entire family emotionally, physically and financially.

To begin with, I recommend her to take a healthy diet and exercise regularly. At the outset of this, she exclaims her inability to go for a walk or a jog because of:

(i)   Lack of time as she has to spend the majority of her time to take care of everyone else in the family.

(ii)   In the rural areas and remote villages, women are not comfortable to go for a walk alone because they don't feel safe and are quite concerned about the on lookers. In other words, they feel shy. This exists even in semi-urban areas where women of certain communities think of leaving the house for physical activity as a taboo. Establishing women friendly parks may benefit such circumstances.

(iii) She eats whatever is left over and does not prioritize getting her nutritional needs met because she says, "If the children are well fed, I am content". When you are travelling in an aircraft, in case of suspected emergency landings or turbulence people are advised to wear the masks themselves first and then aid the person sitting next to them. Similar principle applies for our day-to-day life as well. She should be encouraged and motivated to take care of herself first. Only then will she be able to tend to her kids and family.

(iv) Taking care of herself is often considered as being "selfish" and such behaviour is not appreciated by those around her. She must be rewarded and commended everytime she does an act of self-love so she indulges in that behaviour more. She should understand that taking care of oneself is not a luxury but a necessity.

(v) Discourage the "altruistic" concept around which she has built her life on. She believes she has to live for her children and husband. The narrative should be changed as, "You have to live for yourself first" and then everything else can follow.

(vi) Most women are still concerned about, "What will the others say?" An honest response to that question is – Nobody really gives a damn about us. Each of them has their own miserable life to worry about.

Why did the women's mind come to evolve to this kind of thinking?

For thousands of years, women were oppressed and subjected to social inequalities. They were deprived of basic human rights. In India, women gained rights over property in the 20th century due to the efforts made by various political leaders among whom our ex chief minister **Mr. Karunanidhi** played a vital role. This means that until then only the sons would inherit ancestral property and any land could be registered only under a man's name. But around the 20th century this law was renounced, and new laws came into force where women had equal rights to own wealth. Before this, the societal structure that prevailed until then saw women as burdens of the society and treated them as "no" important. This culture is prevailing even today and women are regarded as market materials to be sold off at marriage and men are sold to the highest bidders as they are considered as prized possessions. Men ask for dowry shamelessly and think they are worthy just because of their gender. This can be seen as official long-term prostitution where men are sold for a good price.

In order to generate a progressive reasonable society children must be taught that the value of people should not be a measure of their material wealth but on the virtues they possess.

Even today many well qualified people have this cerebration. When it comes to assessing a person's worth – it is only possible by dividing them into 2 groups. They are:

1. <u>High value people</u> – people who are kind, compassionate, loyal, empathic, genuine, authentic and people of integrity, they see you for who you are as a person. Such things cannot be seen or counted.

2. <u>Low value people</u> – people who ask questions like
    (i)   How much money you have?
    (ii) How many rooms does your house have?
    (iii) What car do you drive?
    (iv) How costly is your school bag?
          Their focus is on things that you can count. When it comes to things like money that can be counted, it becomes a never-ending quest because the upper limit of numbers is infinity. So, no matter how much money a person has, there is always going to be one other person who has one paisa more. The value assigned pertaining to money is ambiguous and is ever changeable. Hence, it is not wise to rely on such an elusive metric.

Women feel more responsible than men over their kids' well-being and academic prowess. This instills a feeling of guilt in the mothers where they personalise,

"My child is not doing well because of me, I gave birth to the child and hence it is COMPLETELY my responsibility". We all should come to a combined agreement that bringing up kids is a collective responsibility of the entire community and it does not dwell upon a single individual. Lately, this collective responsibility has shrunk owing to **hyper individualistic societies** that have been influenced from the West. Aunts and uncles, grandparents and cousins are no longer in the purview of children's growth and it has become", Everyone for themselves". This kind of hyper-individualistic society will breed more psychiatric conditions like psychosis.

In medicine there are 4 levels of prevention of any illness. This kind of hyper-individualistic society will:

1. <u>Primordial prevention:</u> This is directed at the general population. Everyone including healthy people are the targets for primordial prevention. This focusses on reducing the risk factors for a certain disease that prevail in the community. For example, we advise people to consume more vegetables and exercise regularly to reduce the chances of them developing diabetes.

2. <u>Primary prevention:</u> This is also targeted at healthy individuals but refined to cater to those who are at an increased risk of developing an illness. For example, all children are given compulsory vaccinations to prevent developing fatal infectious diseases.

3. <u>Secondary prevention:</u> This is targeted at people who have already acquired/developed an illness. Steps to reduce the suffering like early detection, rendering easy access to treatment etc. are the strategies under this type of prevention.

4. <u>Tertiary prevention:</u> This is done in the form of rehabilitation and helping patients with disease to gain a normal functioning life as possible. For example, giving physiotherapy for a patient with paralysis is a type of tertiary prevention.

5. <u>Quaternary prevention:</u> This is targeted at patients who have the disease but are not ill i.e., reducing the unnecessary over prescription of medicines that have potential side effects which maybe more harmful than the benefits it is purported to convey.

Considering all the above, the most efficient way of reducing the mental health burden will be implementing the "Primordial Prevention", because once you develop a mental illness, unfortunately, (I hate to say this) you will have to continue taking medicines for a substantial amount of time and deal with all its effects and side effects.

Hence the best strategy is "Primordial Prevention".

"வரும் முன் காப்போம்".

The best ways to implement this is to advice healthy diet, exercise and promote active socialization. It is as simple as that. There is no need for unique fancy Freudian terms or clinical skills. If there is a disequilibrium in any of the above said entities then there is a higher chance of incurring mental illness.

Each state should take up the responsibility of executing these plans in the schools. This is a "must" because primordial prevention of mental health issues should start from school as that is the period of maximal brain development. Healthy adults come from healthy younger version of themselves and not through penancing to any super-natural spiritual entity that costs you an elephant. If this is followed, then in the next 20 years we will have an entire generation of healthy resilient adults who can foster similar beings. The lifestyle that such healthy adults would spin for themselves will be much different from the current corporate lifestyles that we all despise.

If the current life trend goes unchecked, then our future generations are sure to have a therapist for them for their entire life or they would opt to become a therapist themselves.

People are becoming experts in personality tests and reflecting on childhood trauma. This is the outcome of a society that has been through a lot of troubles with each of its member having the feeling of "Nobody has ever understood me", yet everyone wants to be understood, and nobody ever makes an attempt to understand the other person. This is a dysfunctional mentality that is a culture medium for hostility and loneliness. If you have a single person in your life who GETS you and who can stand by you no matter what, then you are indeed very lucky. If the hyper individualistic society concept (where you must deal with everything yourself, be strong, "You got this" captions) continues to grow, then even finding that one person is going to be a challenge.

I am against the "You got this" (உன்னால் முடியும்)" caption because it turns the entire responsibility of creating peace and happiness to the hands of that person who is suffering.

It can be better said as "We got this (நம்மால் முடியும்)", so we as a community are pitching in for another person and makes that person understand that they need not have to go through that alone. Life is difficult already and nobody should be allowed to face it all alone.

The Rich Entitled Generation

Post independence, with the fruitful efforts of our forefathers and socio-political fighters, a large chunk of our population has gained access to education and through that has gained a certain degree of economic advantage where they can afford food, shelter, clothing and a decent amount of money to invest.

With rapid growth in technology and the ease of access to education, we are now witnessing Himalayan growth among people from socially and economically deprived backgrounds which is indeed a pleasure to see.

But it has a downside!

The children of such people, who are "the entitled generation" are now living their lives as reckless adventure seeking spendthrifts. It is not entirely their fault because their parents who have literally built themselves up from scratch have at some point failed to teach "values and virtues that matter" and instead subconsciously instilled in them the feelings of pleasure through "immediate gratification". This is a deadly strategy because soon these kids will value only money and the things that can be quantified. They will be oblivious to human connection and suffering. Their future will be at jeopardy.

Case scenario

A beautiful 15-year-old girl born to a high achieving single mom, is now refusing to appear for her Board exams as she is of firm conviction that she will get married to a rich guy and settle in life. So, she does not go to school, hangs out with her friends in the so called "cool" parties where she hopes there is a possibility of meeting a rich kid and falling in love.

Given the odds, this child has a hard time adjusting with her mother at home. Maybe the relationship she has with her mother is estranged. Given this situation, a healthy self-respecting mind will yearn to become financially independent as soon as possible so they can flee from the distressing home situation.

On the contrary, this child is planning on moving from one hell to her own perceived version of heaven which can prove to be any type of hell or heaven. This is an uncertainty that this child is building her entire future on. She is basically building castles in thin air – to be honest I don't know if this will work or not. She may actually end up meeting her soulmate at 16 and get married to him, I don't know!

<u>But the pitfalls in her plan are:</u>

(i) Falling in love with a rich kid – if a rich kid falls for her, what is the probability that he will stay committed to only her? If he strays around, is she okay with living such a life?

(ii) <u>Getting married to him</u> – what are the odds that the guy whom she fell in love with at 15 years might eventually turn up to be her husband?

(iii) <u>Staying with him</u> – given her temperament and laid-back attitude about life, will she be able to adjust to her new home with her husband and in laws?

(iv) <u>Living as a dependent all her life</u> – as she has not planned on earning a living, she is signing up for a life of complete dependency on her husband for basic survival. *Whoever you are in a relationship with and whatever be the nature of the relationship, if you don't add value to their life, you will lose your value and will be doomed to live a life losing your self-respect. This is not advisable from mental health and social equality points of view.* This will culminate in low self-esteem and the person will finally land up in depression.

(v) If that marriage breaks due to whatever reason, what is her plan B?

(vi) Despite all this, there is also a miniscule probability of her living the life of a rich wife which I would say is simply a wonderful stroke of luck!!

And what about the boys?

The sudden rise of drug abuse and increased rates of rapes in the country are in part a reflection of the untamed precious "male child". Money and power can do things we can never imagine. It is imperative we put it all to good use and to the prosperity of humanity.

THE PROBLEMS IN CHILDHOOD

Just like adults, children too suffer from a range of mental illnesses. I am not going to share the diagnostic criteria of all the mental disorders but will share the common symptoms that the parents and teachers can pick from kids.

Anxiety

When we think of the evolution of emotions of all species, fear and anxiety was the first to come. This fear was of survival benefit for each species because sensing threat and reacting to it within few milliseconds helped them evade predators and increased their rates of survival. While we were hunter gatherers we were always at the risk of being eaten by a wild animal. Our reflexes sharpened and got refined over the years by increasing the fear response and reacting in an appropriate manner. So, whenever you feel intense fear, it is a sign that you are switching to "survival mode" of living. This has to be addressed as early as possible because exaggerated fear leads to the development of "Anxiety disorder" which means your cortisol (stress hormone) level is going to be permanently elevated until the situation changes. Once the situation changes and leads to a favorable outcome, the cortisol level drops, leading to a reduction in anxiety and equilibrium prevails.

But what if the situation does not change or takes longer (say 2-3 years) to change or changes and results in an unfavourable outcome?

In practical life, we are going to be facing umpteen challenging situations and the fluctuating cortisol level is going to play havoc with the brain. We may ask what are children going to be anxious about? They got no bills to pay nor bosses to answer to. A child's world is unique and it has its own set of fears and worries.

Not all fear is a disorder. For example, we study hard so we don't fail the exams. Here the fear of failing makes us study and not waste time. A limited amount of fear is an essential driving force for our survival and to achieve our dreams.

If this fear is exaggerated, in a way that it cripples our functioning to an extent that whenever I open the book, I imagine I am going to fail and that prevents me from concentrating and reading, it results in what we call "Anxiety Disorder".

Such anxiety is not only limited to exams, it extends to other life events also. Some kids may be afraid of the dark, of crossing the roads, of seeing strangers, of going to school, of food, or it can be anything. This should become a cause of concern if the fear cripples the basic functioning that is required of the child – going to school, involving in healthy social interactions, studying, maintaining self-care, having healthy food etc. If nothing else is hampered, then the child can be encouraged to gain self-esteem in other forte so the confidence developed in one area if strong enough will pervade into all other areas of the child's personality and will mitigate all kinds of fear and hinder it from developing into an Anxiety disorder.

<u>Other symptoms of anxiety disorder that we can see:</u>

1. Undue sweating.
2. Shaking of the hands, trembling voice when talking.
3. Sweaty palms.
4. Reacting promptly without giving time to process what happened.
5. Awareness of one's own heart-beat.
6. Frequently using the toilet (for passing urine and/ or motion).
7. Always having a feeling that something might go wrong.
8. Worrying over the mundane things of life.
9. An exaggerated pause when spoken to or when questioned by the teacher in class (here this time is taken to contain the anxiety and to gain composure to be able to answer the question) despite knowing the answer very well.
10. Passing urine in bed in the night after being dry at night for a few months.
11. Bluntly refusing to go to school claiming to be sick or having a stomach- ache and suddenly becoming alert playing at home after 9 am (the time after which going to school is not possible).

    These are some of the common symptoms seen in kids and if you think your kid may be having an anxiety disorder, kindly consult the nearest psychiatrist because you might have to go for few regular sessions and it is more convenient having a therapist nearby so the treatment is adequately followed up. Kids open up to people whom they feel comfortable with and it is difficult on the children's end if you take them to a new therapist each time because they will again have to warm up to the new doctor each time, tell the whole story again. This is time consuming and is less likely to benefit.

Fear of each entity has its own unique fancy name and knowing that is not going to free you of your suffering. Refrain from reaching out to google and spend your energy on how you and your child can overcome it.

The proud anxious person

Some people claim they are anxious and are quite proud of it. This is usually a mask worn by narcissists to easily manipulate you and get things their way. Anxious people are a bit embarrassed by their difficulties and try to cover it up as much as they can. They don't boast about their flaw. Beware of the one who is claiming to be anxious because they are covering something else up.

How to deal with anxiety?

The treatment is of two kinds:

1.   Using medicines.
2.   Using talking therapy.

Which mode to use for who is decided by the combined agreement between the client and the therapist. There is no one size fits all. For kids, the treatment strategy, the counselling technique is entirely different from that for adults. When anxious children are effectively treated they will grow up to become high achieving adults who go on to excel in their chosen fields. Please don't think that "My child is perfect and does not need a therapist" and nip a potential in its bud that has the propensity to become a complete beautiful garden by itself.

<u>The difficulties of a child with anxiety disorder:</u>

1. Poor in studies
2. Not eating or sleeping well
3. Decreased interaction with others

The most disabling handicap in today's age:

Children who are anxious will chose a career that does not involve mingling with others -> they will work in isolation -> decreased interaction with others -> no social circle -> no networking -> they cannot grow career wise without having the necessary connections/strings to pull -> end up in unfulfilling careers, wallowing in self-pity, living a life of regrets wondering, "If only someone had helped me cope with my anxiety, my life would have turned different".

Depression

Adults tend to think kids these days start cribbing at the drop of a hat. There is a widespread belief that today's kids are entitled and are having it very easy tiding through a life of comfort. No doubt that the forthcoming generations will not have to wage wars that we had to face because that is the way of life where the preceding generations make it easier for the next generations. For example, our parents wanted us to live better lives than themselves and we as parents now, are struggling to make our kids' lives easier. By easy, we only mean a life of physical comfort and monetary growth.

Our grandfather rode a bicycle, our fathers rode a motorbike and we are riding our own cars. This is seen as growth and development as it can be quantified easily and understood by all irrespective of socio-educational-economic status. What is invisible is the development and importance of "Emotional Intelligence" in the successive generations. Everyone has a "mind", and every mind has a tendency to develop mental illness including depression.

Adults get frustrated at the fact that these kids become depressed and suicidal for asking to get their hair cut. We should teach our kids that "Depression" which is a clinical diagnosis is different from the feeling of sadness which they feel. All kinds of sadness are mislabeled as depression which irks us all.

What is depression?

A feeling of pervasive sadness which causes defective functioning in all areas of life including at work, social and interpersonal life. This means the child will not be able to study, not talk to classmates, has decreased or no interest in everything even watching movies or going to restaurants, profound lack of cheer and a feeling of tiredness all the time. But these may differ from child to child and all these may not be present at all times. In most children, depression presents itself as getting irritable for minor things, being forgetful, endless doom scrolling of social media etc.

What happens when a usually high performing child becomes clinically depressed?

They lose their ambition which may then seem as too difficult to pursue and find other easier courses and jobs to do. This is because in clinical Depression, the main cognitive functions of attention, concentration and memory are disrupted. So, they are unable to focus on tasks and subjects like math and physics that warrant more attention and cognitive functions. Eventually, they spiral down to low functioning mode or the "battery saving mode" where the brain functions just adequately to bear the perceived difficulties of survival (brushing their teeth, wearing clothes etc.) and has no more resources to imbibe the complexities of Math and Science.

Knowing this, the brain thinks, "Ok I can't study much. Let me find an easy way out... let me settle at whatever job I get".

Hence, they engage in doom scrolling which does not require much of our cognitive faculties in motion.

This is the reason why many children with outstanding performance in school derail from their more intellectual goals and settle down in mediocre jobs. In this stage, the brain loses its awareness of decreased potential. They believe that they are a failure and think that is the life they are given. This is what we call as "Insight" in psychiatry.

In most mental health disturbances, people suffering from it have no realization that they have a mental illness because the brain which is the organ that is responsible for "self-awareness" is not functioning in full capacity and hence the resulting loss of Insight.

Sometimes, kids never vocalise that they feel low or sad and just go about living day to day life suffering in silence. These are "high risk" scenarios where the illness might have motivated the brain to seek alternative routes like suicide or exposure to drugs.

Parents tend to think "We have given them food, good education, we buy them whatever they ask for, what is there for them to become depressed about?"

Like I have said before, mental illness sees no partiality.

"மன நோய் பாரபட்சமே பார்க்காது. யாருக்கு வேணாலும் வரலாம்".

Depression does not come with terms and conditions. Anyone can become depressed. I don't know how many of you know this, but the Bollywood style icon and actress

Deepika Padukone had suffered from Major Depressive episode at one point in her life. Since then, she is running an organization that helps people battling depression. So, I would like you all to imagine, if Deepika Padukone – who has seemingly gotten it all in her life (from the third person's point of view), can become depressed then you and I are no exceptions, nor is your child.

<u>Other symptoms of depression in children:</u>

1. Becoming angered easily.
2. Picking up fights with peers for small things.
3. Difficulty with sleep or sleeping all the time.
4. Craving junk food.
5. Doom scrolling.
6. Changes in appetite.
7. Isolating self.
8. Becoming tearful easily.
9. Losing things and being forgetful.
10. Acting as if "I don't care".
11. Talking about death or more about the past.
12. Laughing at small things that none of their peers find funny.
13. Having difficulty passing motion, or frequent urination.
14. Failing in tests.
15. Considered as being "arrogant" and "disobeying" suddenly as opposed to their compliant older self.
16. Excessive pre-occupation with sex and bodily parts that is out of proportion to age, maturity and exposure level.

17. Becoming more adamant.
18. Sometimes they may seem "NORMAL" and yet be depressed!

The best way out is to build a healthy lifestyle where we reduce the risk factors that promote the development of a depressive mind. Like previously discussed, the foremost methods are to encourage everyday physical activity and include high fibre diet. Once the illness sets in, please don't hesitate to consult a psychiatrist.

As parents, most of them hesitate to consult a psychiatrist because they think, "My child is alright. He/she doesn't need a therapist telling him/her what to do".

It is easier for parents to believe that

"My child is behaving this way wantedly"

– *"என் புள்ள வேணுனே பன்றான்".*

rather than admitting,

"My child is mentally ill"

– *"என் பிள்ளைக்கு மன நோய்".*

If they go to a psychiatrist, then it is them admitting to themselves and to the world that something is "Wrong" with their child. Because of their reluctance to seek professional help, the child is suffering the wrath of a delayed diagnosis and treatment. It is time to set aside our preconceived myths and conceptions about mental health, gain clarification about what our child is going through and to seek help whenever necessary.

OCD

It stands for obsessive compulsive disorder. This has two components:

1. <u>Obsessions</u> – it can be a thought, an image flashing in the mind or it can be an impulse to do something that is not comforting. It causes extreme distress to the individual because these thoughts or images are not desirable by the person. For example, some kids get thoughts that are of sexual nature concerning their parents and it is extremely disgusting to them. They try to stop this thought but fail eventually and suffer in silence for fear of being ridiculed by the society for developing these thoughts in the first place. These thoughts are repetitive and highly intrusive (*ஊடுருவும் தன்மை கொண்ட சிந்தனைகள்*) in the sense it would come up in the mind anytime of the day – when you're in a meeting, when studying for the exam or while writing or even while bathing. Little do the friends and family know that the person suffering from this problem has no control over the origin or maintenance of these thoughts. They have absolutely no control over this and in some but not all severe cases, they think suicide is the only way out because these thoughts arise from within

the head and no matter how hard the person tries they cannot get rid of the thoughts or their head. The most common obsession we see in the community is the "fear of contamination". Here the person harbouring this fear believes that their hands are dirty, they keep washing it over and over again despite everyone else telling them that their hands are clean yet they are not satisfied. So, this behaviour continues unabated to an extent they spend an enormous amount of time ascertaining cleanliness that they miss going to work/school on time, have difficulty meeting target at work/school due to excessive time spent in the restroom washing, unable to keep up with their social life for fear of getting contaminated from the restaurants or movie theatres. It can be disabling and the worst part is nobody would ever understand.

2. <u>Compulsions</u> – These are behaviours that an individual engages in, inorder to negate the distress caused by obsessions with a belief that it would nullify the distress and the effects of the undesirable thought or image that arose. It can be an external behaviour (like repeatedly washing hands over and over again) or an internal behaviour (like praying for forgiveness for getting sexual thoughts about parents). The mind is satisfied to a certain extent for a limited time and then again, the distressing thought recurs. So, the compulsive behaviour tends to get repeated, and

the person is not satisfied as the obsession creeps up again.

A case scenario

She was an 11 years old girl, studying 6th standard with both her parents running the family business. She has a younger brother 9 years old studying in 4th standard. Her parents were fully engrossed in their family run garment business that they had no time to tend to their kids. The kids just grew. She was brought to me because she had refused to go to school for the past 7 months. She was otherwise healthy. She was quite a high performing child in school, always standing first in class, had a good group of friends. Her parents could not pick out a single reason on why she refused to go to school. Initially they were of the opinion that it was just a transient phase and soon she would be back bringing her "A" game. As months passed by, the school management had called the parents and told them that if she continues to miss school, she will have to be retained in the same standard as she has missed a substantial number of classes. The parents who were worried rushed to my clinic to get their daughter evaluated.

As I spoke to her, I realized that she was an intelligent inquisitive child, was interested in astrophysics and loved her parents despite their chronic absence from her life. Times like this make me wonder being a hands-on parent is not that difficult after all. Only two principles must be met when it comes to parenting –

(i) <u>Sense of Certainty (நிச்சயத் தன்மை)</u>: A feeling of certainty that "My parents are there for me no matter what".

(ii) <u>Sense of Security (பாதுகாப்புத் தன்மை)</u>: A feeling of safety in this unpredictable world that "My parents will go to any extent to protect me".

It is these two virtues that must be instilled in our children's minds and if that is achieved, we have succeeded as parents. To all the parents out there, it is nobody's business to comment on how good a parent you are. We are all trying our best to give our kids a happy childhood. As long as your child says, "You are the best mother/father", you need not worry or doubt your parenting skills, I am sure you are doing an amazing job. Not everyone is going to understand your life choices because people understand only from their level of perception.

Given the circumstance of the parenting in this situation discussed, the parents were not really around but they ensured a feeling of security and certainty in their kids – which was exactly why she was able to excel in her studies, have a good healthy gang of friends except over the last 7 months.

Then she slowly opened up saying that she was worried something dreadful might happen to her parents and the only way to prevent it was by staying close to them so she can prevent anything untoward happening to them. This fear of "harm befalling parents/caretaker" is the most common manifestation of OCD in kids and in her case, it has crippled her from going to school. This behaviour of refusing school is the "Compulsion" that she has developed to ensure her parents' safety.

What causes OCD?

There are several theories that implicate the imbalance of the neurotransmitter – Serotonin (a chemical in the brain), for the origin of many mental health issues including OCD.

What is the cause of this imbalance?

Nobody really knows! What we know for sure is how to treat the imbalance and ensure complete recovery of the person suffering from it. Please consult a nearby psychiatrist if you think you or your child is suffering from this disorder.

Tics

A tic is a sudden physical bodily movement or a vocal sound or the uttering of a particular word that a person does repeatedly and has no control over it. This is also a type of OCD that is often made fun of by peers and ridiculed by parents and teachers that frequently results in the kids getting physical punishment. I don't want to go into the specific neural wiring pattern that causes this because even brain scientists are debating on why this happens. The kids who have these symptoms are considered to have "behavioural" problem because the adults in the equation believe that the kids are indulging in such behaviour intentionally and are enjoying the attention they get out of this exhibit. On the contrary, the child goes through tremendous displeasure and tries to control it but it all goes in vain. This is a clinical condition that warrants treatment and other tests to rule out major abnormalities in the brain.

Such disorders are more common in boys than in girls.

He was an 8 years old boy studying in 3rd standard at an International school. He was faring well in his studies and loved taking part in speech competitions where he invariably got the first prize. Over the past three months, he was found to be disobedient in class, "talking and screaming out random words" that didn't make sense to anyone else but when asked what he had said, he said it was a German song that he had recently heard. His parents were terrified of this change of situation and as they were from an affluent background they took all the tests that could ever be done on an 8 year old child including PET scan of the brain. This is a special type of scan that is available only in selected centres in Tamilnadu. The tests showed that everything was normal and the parents were clueless as to why he was saying things out of the blue.

For the next few weeks, they were convinced that he was making these sounds deliberately and started punishing him. This kind of externally imposed stress aggravates the tic and hence he began making more of these sounds. His friends who were all equally young did not understand him and they were advised by his parents to avoid talking to him for fear of them getting the same "problem behaviour".

All over India, parents have a uniform belief -

"My child is good, he/she changed only after becoming friends with this other child".

"இந்த பசங்க கூட சேர்ந்த பிறகு தான் என் புள்ள கெட்டுபோயிட்டான்".

Here I would like to shed light on the fact – the whole society is not compelled to spoil our children. Few factors prevailing in our society may make some kids engage in deviant and unhealthy behaviours, but there is more love in the world out there than we can imagine. Especially the people in Tamilnadu, have strong principles and morals when it comes to children and education – thanks to leaders like Periyar, Ambedkar, Kamarajar, Karunanidhi etc. to mention a few.

With the view of "protecting" their children from acquiring a mental illness that has no route to spread through communication or befriending, all parents tell their kids not to mingle with the child that has unusual behaviour. This isolation further aggravates the tic and makes the boy's life worse.

Finally on recommendation by a teacher, they came to consult me. When I spoke to the child, I understood how painful it was to live in his world. The worse part was when he said, "Nobody even asked me why I was doing this, they just assumed I did it on purpose. Doctor, please believe me, I am not doing it wantedly, it just comes… and goes. I don't know what to do".

When asked about the incomprehensible words that he uttered, he said that the sound he utters is too vulgar and so he has added a few more jargon words to it so it doesn't sound as bad.

Can you guess why this child opened up to me?

Any clue as to why he told me everything on the first session?

I was the only one who asked "**Why?**"

I was spellbound by the Emotional Intelligence of this child. We do have a lot to learn from our children.

Sometimes, maybe seeing the world through a child's eyes may solve most of our problems perhaps.

Please leave the treatment of this condition to an expert and don't waste your time and your child's entire childhood using home remedies that you saw on YouTube. Trust me, if there was any home remedy to treat an established mental illness, I will be the first one to advocate it.

Can it be prevented?

We can, to a certain extent reduce the risk factors that promote the development of mental illness – you know what I am going to say – exercise and regular passing of motion.

The plus side of having this class (OCD and tics) of disorders:

There is a virtue called "conscientiousness" and people with tics or OCD are said to have high conscientiousness.

In Thamizh it is translated as -

"*மனசாட்சி*".

This means that Such people when studied were found to have a very strong sense of right and wrong, high moral values and they held on to principles very dearly in life. They are mostly the dependable ones – someone who can stick to their words, keep up their promises, would not do to others what they wouldn't want to be done to themselves etc. This finding is the result of a few studies and I don't mean to certify every human with OCD or tic to be a perfect human being. There are exceptions to every rule – this finding is to be treated with caution. But just like how I romanticize mental illness, I would like to paint this also, for the world would be a bloody boring place if not for the outliers (for details on outliers please refer to my previous book). There is joy in life and there is a lot of life in diversity.

ADHD

This diagnosis has become a trending word among the new age parents. Many parents come to us with the diagnosis and ask for treatment and counselling. I kindly request all teachers and parents to refrain from making a clinical diagnosis of their own and let the experts do their job. The reason for this is because once you "Label" a child of having some mental illness or disorder, it is going to stay with them for a long time. And nothing fruitful is going to come out of your diagnosis. Let us save the child some freedom and dignity.

This popular acronym stands for "Attention Deficit Hyperactivity Disorder". As the name implies, kids with ADHD have difficulty paying attention to tasks. Attention is defined as the ability to focus on a particular task. There are many types of attention like selective attention, sustained attention, divided attention, alternating attention, executive attention etc. For the purpose of this book, I am not going into details. The basis of the underlying problem is that the child is unable to focus on one particular task at any given time. This inattention is not only restricted to school environment, but also extends to home situations, in the playground etc.

Other commonly experienced symptoms include

1. Difficulty doing homework.
2. Loses things.
3. Makes careless mistakes.
4. Easily forgetful.
5. Not listening when spoken to.
6. Scoring poorly in tests (this is often mistaken by parents to be a problem of memory, as they believe that the child knows the answer but forgets it at the time of the exam and because of this belief they come to us asking for tablets that improve memory. On the contrary, this forgetfulness is due to a lack of attention to subject when it was taught and not a problem associated with memory. For a memory trace to be formed in the brain, first it has to be

   (i)   focused on,
   (ii)   understood,
   (iii)   encoded in the brain,
   (iv)   stored,
   (v)   then retrieved.

In kids with ADHD, the first step of attention itself is impaired hence there is no scope of even testing comprehension and memory which are all the basis of time consuming expensive IQ tests that are just a number and the sole use of it is to claim disability benefits from the state government (here the services rendered by the government to such kids is highly commendable).

ADHD has a hyperactivity part that is frequently observed by parents and teachers. The common symptoms encountered are:

1. Being fidgety.
2. Inability to sit still in class, squirming in the seat.
3. Interrupting when others are talking.
4. Blurting out answers even before the question is completed.
5. Difficult to contain them in a confined space.
6. Breaks/drops things (is bullied as having "butter fingers" by peers).
7. Always on the "go".

It is impossible to miss symptoms of ADHD as it is an overt (externally observable) behaviour.

What causes ADHD?

Just like most mental illnesses the cause has not been identified yet but we have effective treatment strategies. Few research scientists have said that parental smoking or drug abuse can cause ADHD. Some studies show that ultra processed refined foods exacerbate these symptoms but results are inconclusive. No matter what the disease I would always recommend to stick to whole grains and locally sourced fruits and vegetables while avoiding even recreational use of drugs/alcohol.

The cons of not treating ADHD in childhood

1. Though these children have great academic potential, they will under- perform in academics

due to a lack of attention and land up in low achieving careers that are far beneath their means.

2. The ADHD brain is inherently low on a neurochemical called dopamine. This motivates them to seek activities that provide them with immediate pleasure. There are higher chances of these kids developing problems with all kinds of addiction.

3. There are more chances of developing other mental illnesses like depression and bipolar disorder.

The reason why most psychiatrists practice until their last breath is because of the gratification this job provides where we transform lives and make people live a life that they would but couldn't because of a mental illness that has hindered them living a soul fulfilling life all along.

Any mental illness when treated effectively can transform lives. We have seen the metamorphosis of people to beautiful butterflies following treatment and that is what drives me to write this book.

Challenges faced by parents

It is not easy being the parent of a child with certain difficulties. Some teachers happily wash their hands off the kid saying that parents have to move the child to another school that would supposedly accommodate him/her. The parents are helpless because they can't tolerate seeing their one kid going to the best school in town and another kid going to a mediocre school. The teachers' lack of concern is due to their lack of awareness of such a thing as mental illness exists and the fact that it is completely treatable.

When you think about it, the estranged conversations you have with people around you is to a greater degree due to their ignorance and not due to arrogance. This mass ignorance is of emotional origin where most people opine "If it does not affect/bother me, it is fine", whereas the truth behind this is their inability to comprehend the sufferings of others around them and they think just because they have not endured that agony, it is not "important".

I have come across several cold people who proudly claim,

"எனக்குலாம் அப்படி தோணாது பா", when they don't "get" why someone was suffering or understand a patient's perspective.

In other words, most people believe that, *"எனக்கு வந்தா ரத்தம் உனக்குன்னா தக்காளி சட்னி"*.

To those of you who have found yourself proclaiming your proud cognition that "I can control my Mind, I am not weak to get mental illness", – you are simply fortunate to have a brain that is resilient to suffering and it is not because of anything that you proactively constructed throughout your life.

It is most fascinating to see someone who has actually underwent colossal suffering, re-gain their life back from scratch and build an empire out of dust. That is something to be proclaimed with pride and not the callosity that some people were born with. Indeed, some people are incredibly lucky to be bestowed with a brain that can never become depressed or mentally unstable – Well, good for you! But this does not entitle you to make a mockery of those who are suffering.

Autism and Learning Disability

The word "Autism" comes from the Greek word "autos" which means "self". Kids who have been diagnosed with autism have an inwardly directed flow of thoughts and energy. They pay little consideration to the world outside of themselves and have a world of their own in which only "the self" exists. In extreme cases they firmly believe that they are the center of the universe and that the entire world revolves around them. They are incapable of coming to terms with the fact that other people have emotions of their own. Some studies show that these kids also have emotions but the problem lies in identifying and naming them as they have low levels of emotional intelligence. The bright side of this is that emotional intelligence can be taught and developed in these kids with consistent effort. Apart from difficulty in handling emotions in the self and identifying emotions in the others, some of them may also have difficulty in language development. The emotional dysregulation can be identified by a few of the following:

1. Not turning or responding to when called by name even though hearing is intact.
2. Unable to follow a conversation.
3. Difficulty maintaining eye contact when spoken to.

4. Unable to mingle with other kids and have co-operative play.

5. Hitting others.

6. Unable to share joy or pain. (For example, when a child is appreciated in class, usually he/she comes home excited about it and shares the event with their family members, where as kids with autism don't share emotional things like this).

7. When you've had a bad day, and it is so obvious in your face but your child coming from school fails to ask you "What's wrong mom?"

8. They are engrossed in their own world playing with a few specific toys in an unusual way. (Playing with a toy car by simply spinning its wheels with fingers rather than riding it on the floor in the usual way).

9. Indulging more in spinning movements of the body like twirling around, rocking back and forth etc.

10. Seeking pleasure from soft toys, paying unusual attention to texture of things rather than the purpose for which it is intended to be used.

11. Involving in more self-talk than the kids of same age.

Cause of autism

Many parents are of the opinion that not engaging with the child in the toddler period is the sole cause of autism. Working parents who find it convenient to leave their kids with their grandparents internalize a lot of guilt and blame themselves which results in either of the parents (usually the mother) quitting their job and becoming a stay at home parent. While I cannot emphasize enough the need to engage with your children right from when they are conceived inside the womb, it is not your fault that your child has developed autism. Autism is a neuro developmental disorder. This means the disorder has begun right from when the child was conceived. The intricate neuronal branching (which cannot be identified by any imaging or blood tests) is at fault and there is unfortunately nothing you can do about it. IT IS NOT YOUR FAULT. Many reasons cannot be explained by science and this is one such thing.

Autism is not a disease to be cured. Kids with autism are just different. Some people have a light brown colored skin, while some people like me have a dark brown colored skin. Being brown is not a disease (another myth that must be busted in India where white skin is worshipped) and hence there is no need to find a magic "cure" for it.

So, what can be done to help children with autism?

There are many therapies devised to help such kids understand emotions and help them navigate through the human experience. These sessions are time consuming but definitely worth it. It requires a lot of patience and resolute to help mould desirable characteristics and cut off undesirable behaviour. There are many therapy centres available in Tamilnadu. It would be helpful if the government establishes such centres where people from all classes of the society may have access to such therapies. We should no longer dread being born poor in India.

What can be done to prevent a child from developing autism?

Some studies show that increasing parental age increases their risk of having kids with autism. However, this result must be approached with caution as there is no absolute truth in psychiatry. All research studies must be approached with caution.

I hate to say this but the answer to this question is "Nobody really knows!"

Contrary to the popular opinion it is not because you went to work immediately after delivery. In such cases, children may have slight delays in speech and have less cheer, but certainly not develop autism. For autism to develop, the neuronal migration during the development of the brain must be faulty and that happens well when your child is inside your womb. I am saying this only to remove the guilt that you endure and I am not advising all parents to abandon their children soon after delivery. The childhood is the golden period for maximal brain development and we should not lose diamonds while hunting for gold.

Learning disability/intellectual disability/mental retardation:

All of these problems show up in primary or middle school.

Specific learning disability

In this type of disorders, kids even though they have normal intelligence, have difficulty with learning specific subjects like reading, writing or mathematics. The most common among them is having difficulty in mathematics. Depending on the level of difficulty and the need of math for their survival, kids can be given extra coaching hours or can be enrolled in academic programs where math is excluded, and another subject is taken up in its place so the kid can gain enough knowledge to make a living despite the handicap. Such novel academic practices are lacking in Tamilnadu and it is high time we create a new curriculum that is inclusive of every kid while creating equal opportunities for all them to earn a living with dignity.

For difficulties in reading and writing the same approach can be followed.

There is a condition called, "Dyslexia", in which kids have difficulty in reading because of abnormal wiring in the brain where they are not able to identify letters, combinations etc. Such kids can be coached to be able to read better with adequate training. I personally know a doctor in the UK who has dyslexia, who is now holding one of the top administrative positions in his field of expertise. So having dyslexia can be challenging but it does not deprive you of achieving any of your dreams. It is going to be a tough task, but if everything was easy it wouldn't really be fun, would it?

Intellectual Disability/ Mental Retardation

To put it in simple words, this is a condition where people do not have the ability to think, decide and operate according to their chronological age.

Kids are said to have Intellectual Disability when they are not able to function like their peers on intellectual, emotional and social level. All this can be spotted easily when a child fails the basic that is expected of them. The following when present in children, should raise concern:

1. Not able to comply to general rules because of a lack of understanding of what is being told to them.
2. Persistently refusing to do something even though it is an easy task.
3. Clumsy movements.
4. Inability to maintain self-hygiene despite being told and demonstrated what to do and how to do.
5. Easily becoming the target of bullying and unable to defend themselves.
6. Frequently refusing to go to school because they are being made fun of and the kids are not able to give an appropriate reason for their refusal.

Like I have already mentioned before, parents of such kids usually ask for memory tablets thinking that their kids are forgetting and that is the reason for all their difficulties. It is not an issue of memory but one of decreased intelligence.

When the topic of intelligence is discussed, we must not miss talking about the elephant in the room.

The older definition of intelligence – the ability to understand, analyse a problem and be able to solve it efficiently. This is the reason why all IQ tests have complex problems of increasing severity with increasing age. This is only a number for reference by the academic institutions for recruiting help for the concerned child and to be able to better accommodate the child in the school setting and help them procure employment.

Apart from this, these IQ tests and the IQ value is of absolutely no use. The latest definition of intelligence is pretty simple and legit!

It is **"The ability to adapt"**. That's it.

Have you noticed the cockroach in your kitchen or garden? Ever wondered for how many years it has been around? They have been in vogue since the dinosaur era. The reason for their impeccable evolution and sustenance is their ability to adapt to various surroundings and harsh environments. Their exoskeleton is perfected to survive a wide range of drought and famine.

Having said that, the take home message here is you don't have to solve Einstein's equation to prove your intelligence. You just have to learn to co-exist with others while trying your best to add value to your life and to those of others around you. If you are living a life like that, then you are one of the few intelligent people the world has seen!

The term "mental retardation" is an older term that was used to describe intellectual disability but is no longer in use now.

There are many severities of intellectual disability like mild, moderate, severe and profound. This classification must be used purely to classify children so that we can plan what type of therapies and help they need to be able to function as much independently as possible and not as a means of derogation, for life is even more difficult for them than it is for "the apparently normal" kids.

Parents, especially Indian parents should be encouraged to develop a thick skin to the naysayers. Even in today's age there are people who are worried about,

"What will the others think? What will our relatives say?"

Truth be told, nobody really gives a damn about you or your kid. In this **"Narcissist filled selfie era"**, people are more concerned about themselves than ever before. When I say it's a "Narcissist filled Selfie Era", I want you all to think about the different phases of photographs that has evolved and decide for yourself. I am not implying blind obedience from my readers to everything that I say. In the initial period of "photo taking", we (humans) were all taking pictures of those near and dear to us. We seldom took pictures of ourselves. The process of taking a photograph was a big deal and not everyone deserved to be on our camera roll where we had to pay extra pennies for those extra photos (to those of you who existed in the 90s and before that, know that there were entities called "a camera negative film roll"). To those of you who don't know what this is, please google. Even if we could afford all the negative film rolls, we took more pictures of places and other people rather than of the self.

Over the next few decades, everyone has a camera in their hands at all times which contains at least a thousand photos of themselves, all photos looking strikingly similar, but with subtle differences which only the self can spot out. The more and more attention that is directed towards the self, the more narcissistic the mind becomes, which magnifies the self-zooming glass while reducing the attention to the others.

As this self-love expands, the "others" really don't have the time to think and ponder about your life as opposed to their own life. We should break such toxic ties with the society and re-build healthy ties where we nurture and enrich each other to become the happiest versions of themselves.

Conduct Disorder

A child is said to have "Conduct Disorder" when he/she has a predominant lack of empathy for other's sufferings. This means the child will behave as if nobody else can experience pain or suffering.

Such kids are of the belief that only they are the most important person in this whole wide world (for themselves and for the others as well). Their minds have a gross inability to feel any emotion in depth because of a faulty wiring in their brain. This faulty wiring prevents them from developing "empathy" i.e., the capacity of the brain to understand the pain and emotions of others. So, they behave in a reckless manner doing whatever pleases them and do not care about the impacts of their actions on the others around them.

Reason for evolution of this lack of empathy

<u>The children most commonly diagnosed to have conduct disorder have the following characteristics:</u>

1. They are usually from either a very poor or a very rich background, but this rule is not always true, there tend to be exceptions.
2. They usually have an absent/distant father.

3. Addiction to any type of drug/alcohol is present either in the kids themselves or in any of the family members.

4. It is also co-existent with frequent lying, stealing money from home, or other things from others at school or in relative's houses.

5. The lack of empathy before it extends as cruelty towards other people, it shows itself as cruelty towards animals in childhood as the animals (in their infant days) are tiny helpless creatures that cannot retaliate when harmed. My heart pains even as I write this!

6. There is massive disrespect towards rules and regulations and disobedience towards elders but this point is one of the many behaviours and should not be solely relied upon for diagnosis. This is because given the current socio-political scenario, every rule must be thoroughly analysed and studied before blindly complying and this habit must be cultivated right from childhood where children are encouraged to ask questions and given the freedom to act upon their own free will as long as it does not harm/hurt the self or others.

7. Finally, such kids are prone to frequently cut classes and abscond from school, and return to home at the same time as they would when returning from school.

There are a few postulated theories to explain the evolution of conduct disorder:

In situations where the parents are not being "real parents" kids develop a mind that is thick and callous to pain because they don't have a "go to" person in dire circumstances. By "real parents" I mean, parents who do not provide a sense of security and certainty as explained in the previous chapter.

In these circumstances, when a child is faced with an adversity, and there is no "secure parent figure" to provide comfort, the child's brain which is unable to bear the pain and suffering, creates a shield around itself which is impenetrable to suffering. When the mind creates this shield, it becomes impenetrable by the suffering of the others as well.

In other words, when children don't have that safe spot to seek when in discomfort, they turn their brains into pain-free brains where even though they are in pain, they remain oblivious to the effects of it. This is a survival mechanism for the species – according to Darwin's theory of "Survival of the Fittest" i.e., those that are stronger can survive while others perish. What happens here is, in order to deal with the harsh circumstances during the initial period of growth and development -the brain remodels itself so it can continue to grow while also being able to deal with the hardships. Hardships or harsh circumstances are entirely subjective and it does not mean only "poverty". It can also mean a rich home where there is plenty of food and money but no love. When the brain develops this zone of "Impenetrance" to all the suffering around, it also becomes impenetrable to the suffering of the others. The worst part is such kids even when they grow up to become adults, never develop insight into their disorder and continue to live a life making it difficult for themselves as well as for others.

Apart from this, there are also various genes involved in the development of this disorder. This is the reason why this disorder runs in families. It is more commonly found in boys than in girls.

Is it treatable?

I wouldn't use the word "treatable" but it can be managed to a certain extent and such kids can be bred to become functional members of the society with proper therapy and counselling.

What happens if they go forward untreated?

They develop the adult version of conduct disorder called the "Anti-social personality disorder", where the same behavioural pattern persists but physical cruelty is replaced by manipulative strategies and gas lighting, addiction to drugs/alcohol etc.

In which jobs would these kids prosper?

If such kids are brought up with an academic inclination, they can make excellent professions in the administrative services, nurses, doctors, police and military etc. where there is witnessing of monstrous sufferings and in some situations people with empathy can succumb to their emotions and make faulty decisions and judgements, but those with a callous brain can be trained to do exactly what is needed at that situation without yielding to the emotional turmoil because they cannot really experience the turmoil. This does not imply those with enhanced empathy are going to be terrible at these kind of jobs, for example I am someone with tremendous empathy and this aspect has only made me better than the others at my job, because I have something that others cannot simply learn from a textbook. So... every coin has two sides to it.

Oppositional Defiant Disorder

This disorder was included in the "Diagnostic and Statistical manual of mental disorders" in the 1980s.

The predominant criteria in this disorder is "disobeying" elders, frequently questioning the norms and deliberately doing the opposite of what is told just to spite the others.

In the initial few years following this, in the great USA, most of the kids diagnosed with ODD were of the black race.

??????????????????

If you had guessed correctly, I am strictly against using this as a diagnosis. The above fact conveys the widespread mentality that "Black kids" (or any minority) must be expected to obey and conform and never ask questions; if they had questions then they were labelled as having a "mental illness".

If we were never encouraged to ask questions none of the science or math would have evolved up to where we are now. We may forage into Mars (the red planet) anytime now and it is the question of "why not" that has heralded such drastic growth.

Do you know why the Western countries are considered developed and India is still a developing country?

The "Why"s that the Western country asked has terminated into a growing mindset and there was freedom to explore, seek solutions which further resulted in inventions.

While they were busy answering the "Why"s of the world, Indians were busy performing ancient rituals hoping that some supernatural entity will come to save us. I don't mean offense to any single faith or religion but my agony springs up from the fact that we are still forced to follow ridiculous meaningless rules and regulations just because it is "Tradition = that is how it has been done all these years and hence it must continue to be done the same way".

A thriving example of this is the practice of doing random meaningless things that we do in the name of culture and tradition (which were actually never a part of the culture of native Indians). In fact, the people who lived in the Indus valley were far more progressive and inclusive in their culture and laid the basis of education in the ancient world when scholars from all over the world came to our own Nalanda university for education.

Our society would fare much better if we spent more time questioning the things that matter than in performing meaningless rituals.

"அத்து மீறு".

"அடங்க மறு".

Selective Mutism

This is a condition where kids who are eloquent and cheerful at home, but refuse to speak in certain environments especially in school. They become "mute" in certain situations where they feel anxious. The anxiety they feel is so overwhelming that they never speak. This is not very common but common enough that it needs special mention. There are varied causes for this, the most common being fearfulness due to being judged as "inferior or stupid" by the others (teachers and peers). The reasons for this feeling of inferiority can spring up from upbringing by parents who are themselves quite timid in their approach towards life and are worried about, "What if it goes wrong?" even for mundane situations. The aura in the home environment is one which is replete with "anxious thoughts and undue worry of the future" which imbibes the feeling that the world is quite a scary place.

This can be overcome by teaching our kids "courage" or "தைரியம்" that they can do anything they want and also the courage to deal with the consequences of their actions.

This builds strong willed children who go on to live as happy adults no matter what the circumstances because they have the inner grit and valour to deal with whatever life throws at them and hence they need not live in "survival mode"; while their subconscious mind navigates through life seamlessly their conscious mind gets to enjoy day to day life. No matter what virtues you inculcate in your children – like loyalty, kindness, empathy, gratitude, punctuality etc., the most important one is "*தைரியம்*".

Another reason for this condition is that these kids have a low self-esteem. The low self-esteem evolves from constant under achievement in academics and a lack of knowledge that will give a sense of "fulfillment and confidence". In order to overcome this feeling of inferiority and garner self-esteem, the child must first be encouraged to prove to their value to themselves, i.e., you can't feel good about yourself if you keep failing all the tests in school. This does not imply that scoring high marks is the ultimate aim in life. There are people who have a good sense of self-worth despite faring poorly in academics. Detailed discussion about this is beyond the scope of this book.

For children who have selective mutism, and if they are found to perform poorly in their studies, they should first be encouraged and helped to perform better. Once they realise their worth, they lose the fear of being misjudged by others because they know "Who I am" and hence will neither seek nor depend upon validation from the others. This applies to adults as well. Some parents go beyond and appreciate their kids for the miniscule things in life with the hope of instilling confidence and improving self-worth. In the long term, this will prove counter-productive when the kids face the real world and get their self-image tarnished when they finally realise that all that they have "achieved" is nothing compared to the others and fall into a downward spiral of low worth culminating in depression. The appreciation and rewards given to children must be reasonable and in harmony with what is happening in the outside world lest this will result in unrealistic expectations which when left unfulfilled will lead to drastic self-destructive behaviours like addiction to alcohol and other drugs.

Another reason for selective mutism is the undue sensitivity of some children to the strictness of teachers in school. I wouldn't deny the fact that some teachers displace their anger from home onto these helpless school kids who wouldn't react and would oblige to whatever is said without questioning (another aspect in India which should be cut in its budding stage). Here both the teachers and the kids must be taught civic sense where we shouldn't live at the expense of hurting a fellow human being. Teachers are also human beings and they too have a life but this does not entitle them to take out their anger on the innocent kids.

School Refusal

You will be amazed at the reasons for which kids refuse to go to school these days. It can be as menial as "Thamizh teacher scolded me" to as pressing as "someone abused me at school". Whatever be the reason, we should never leave such instances unexplored because we may be overlooking a pressing issue and label it as an "attitude" problem given the era where children soon mature to young adults. Most of the parents seldom make an attempt to understand their child's life and assume they know everything there is to know about the child's life.

Trust me when I say this –

YOU HAVE ABSOLUTELY NO IDEA what is happening in your child's life – unless you hear them say it or observe them close enough to understand it.

Children are not as vocal as adults in expressing their difficulties – for example, if they don't like an uncle who visits often, they may say they don't like the chocolate that that uncle buys for them. Pay attention.

In Indian households, there is a common practice to tell our girl children to change their comfortable home clothes into a fully covered clothing when some "Uncle" comes home. In such state of affairs, that kind of an "Uncle" for whom our girl children are expected to cover themselves up, should never be allowed inside our home in the first place. This is how we teach the concepts of "safety" and "boundaries" to our kids which will help them nurture healthy relationships in their future. Kids are not going to learn from what you preach them, but learn from what you "show" them.

Another common reason for wanting to cut school is being made fun of by the peers. This used to be more but is now decreasing due to the "Flynn" effect. This was described by a scientist Flynn whereby he observed that with successive generations the average IQ of the population increases. This means that your great grandchildren will be more intelligent than you, not because of the increased development of the world but simply because they were born after finer and finer tuning of the genes that make up the functioning of the brain. With increasing intelligence, there is a surge in the emotional intelligence as well. So, the consideration of other's feelings also takes precedence while communicating. But again, this is not the norm, there are always exceptions to every scientific result or evidence.

Let us say that we have explored the reason for a child refusing school. And now we will have to motivate them to go to school.

Most parents end up leaving the child at home with the phone, all the snacks, a TV, a stable internet connection and they leave to work with the hope that magically some heavenly spirit will change their soul and the kids would suddenly say, "Yes! I want to go to school". Parents furnish their kids' life at home with a soothing atmosphere from which separation is painful. I remember when I was a kid, my friends and I would start studying because we were bored and there was nothing inquisitive to occupy our minds with.

While it is pertinent to give our kids a happy home, during times of distress like this (school refusal), we will have to make the home environment as boring as possible, so they feel frustrated at one point and say, "Okay I've had enough of this. I am going to school".

Some parents take a step further and even take their kids on vacations or to their native places with the expectation of giving their children's minds something relaxing so they will forget the stress at school and later want to go to school. Imagine as an adult, I am taking you to Heaven where you can do anything you want and eat and drink and mate to your heart's content. Then if given a choice of returning back to Earth to your old life, would you be thrilled? You would beg to stay back in heaven.

The home environment when away from school is like a heaven for kids and hence as long as everything dances to their tune at home, they are not going to go back to school.

Another "DON'T" is – sitting the child down and advising them presuming they can change their child's mental make-up and make them go to school. The usual advice given in Indian households is the emotionally charged "We are suffering because of you".

"நாங்க அவனோ கஷ்டப்பட்டு உங்கள படிக்க வைக்கிறோம்".

This advice given with the presumption of making their kids realise the pain that they had to endure to make ends meet, only works by instilling a strong sense of guilt in the young minds which in later years of life predisposes them to develop depression. Children can seldom be taught and advised to do something. What works best for them is "behaviour modification".

The first and the foremost thing to do – take away the phone, disconnect the TV, wifi etc.

Make a deal with them – they can get screen time of one hour, if they go to school that day, or else no phone or TV. They can get their favourite meal/snack on Sunday if they go to school for four consecutive days.

This works 100% of the time. Never fails. It may take some time for this tactic to take effect but it will certainly work! No amount of emotional melodrama will work, so please don't waste your time and energy verbalizing your deep- rooted trauma on a helpless child. If you find yourself taking it all on your child, it is probably your own unresolved emotional conflicts, hence please seek help for the same.

Sometimes "over intelligent high-achieving" kids also have difficulty going to school where the curriculum falls far below their capability. They feel bored. In such situations, the parents and teachers should have a meeting together, and then a meeting along with the child, to draft a unique curriculum for the child based on the child's own interests.

While it is necessary to impart appropriate education, it is also essential to give them a social life where they develop a feeling of belongingness. Some kids with extra ordinary IQ have trouble seeking and maintaining qualitative human relationships. They should not be deprived of their social connections.

Bedwetting and Pica

These are two not so very related conditions but listed here together as they are quite direct and easily discernible.

Bedwetting is a term used to describe kids who have gained bladder control over the night already but have suddenly started wetting their beds again. This means they start peeing (passing urine) in their beds during the night after being dry for few months. For this to be diagnosed as a disorder, the child must be 5 years or older and do not have any other mental or physical illnesses. In kids under 5 years of age, this is quite common and is part of normal development as the brain is slow to mature well enough to gain voluntary control over bladder functions.

For this disorder to be diagnosed, kids must have previously already attained bladder control and then after a substantial period, must revert to wetting their bed. This is what should raise concern because for a child whose brain has already achieved the milestone of controlling the bladder while asleep, has now suddenly deteriorated to previous levels of development and we should find out why.

Before jumping on to the psychological causes behind this we must rule out all other physical causes and mental retardation of any severity. Sometimes this bedwetting can be a rare single occurrence which does not need our attention. It needs to be attended to only if it keeps recurring.

<u>Physical causes:</u> the most common cause is a urinary tract infection. This is quite common among children because

1. They don't drink enough water.
2. They hold the urine until they come home in the evening because most girl children opine that the toilets in the schools are not clean.
3. Some teachers do not allow toilet breaks in between the classes so the kids refrain from drinking water which increases the tendency to develop an infection in the urinary tract.

There are bunch of other causes that a pediatrician has an easy eye for. So, please seek the opinion of an expert before making your own diagnosis.

Now, coming to the psychological causes:

This is called "enuresis" another fancy term coined by the doctors to make it more complicated. The most common cause is a – recent onset stressful situation at home or school. Some children who are not capable of or who are not encouraged to express their emotions in a safe and confidential space tend to express their discomfort through such behaviours. This is not a conscious voluntary behaviour rather an unconscious mechanism operating in the deep layers of the mind. So, punishing the children or telling them they are doing it intentionally to spite their parents is not going to help, it will only make the situation worse. Again, when it comes to what kind of stressful situation can trigger them to bed wet, there is no universally accepted reason.

What is "6" for you is actually "9" for me. You will never understand it until you see it from my side!

All said and done, how to handle this?

1. Cultivate the habit of making kids pass urine just before bedtime.
2. Cut down coffee or tea intake.
3. Reduce water intake after 6 pm.
4. Set up an alarm in the middle of the night, when the child can wake up to go to the toilet to void.
5. Encourage adequate physical activity.
6. Instigate kids to verbalise their feelings.
7. Trust must be earned – it does not come for "free". Your kids must feel that they can confide in you no matter what. This trust paves the way for development of healthy future relationships and secure attachment styles. In order to be an ideal parent, we must be "happy". We cannot pour from an empty cup. Before planning kids, plan on how you would be happy.
8. Apart from this, each child needs a specially catered therapy plan depending on age, gender, the problem encountered, family situation etc. Please consult a nearby psychiatrist at the earliest.

PICA – this is the practice of consuming non-edible, non-nutritive substances. For example, if you are a 90s kid, you would have loved eating chalkpiece. I still do occasionally! The problem here is some kids have an intense craving for such items and they cannot resist it and as a result consume it in large quantities. This is quite common in kids with below average intelligence. Other causes include a severe nutritional deficiency especially iron, protein, vitamin B12, low fibre diet etc.

For this condition to be managed, the doctor needs to run some blood tests to see if all is well, if any deficiency it should be managed, then comes the behavioural part of managing this. Mostly kids know that this is a bad habit, so they would have developed a system to perform this in secrecy. We should literally spy around and find out their sly practices, or ask them to be frank in the conversation, check points instilled, then all appreciable behaviour must be rewarded and unacceptable behaviour must be punished.

If the pica still continues, further exploration must be done to find out the cause and address the cause. This is not something that can be done by parents or caretakers at home. A trained eye can spot the problem within 2 minutes that an untrained eye even after years of contemplation can fail to see. Never shy away from seeking help.

Nobody said parenting was easy. We literally sign up for unpredictability at all levels and phases of life when we decide to have kids. Having dependents at home is not easy – it can be a puppy or a child. Everything demands extra time, energy, money and a whole lot of other resources, but the oxytocin surge that it gives and having a reason to wake up every morning is unmatchable and priceless. Oxytocin is the hormone that gives us a feeling of connection and belongingness. Depletion of this results in loneliness and may at times lead on to depression.

Drugs

With the rise of connections across the globe, our children develop friendships and situationships with people from diverse backgrounds. At this point in time, we have no control over their connections. While it is difficult to keep spying on them, it is rather easier to divert their consciousness into seeking higher goals so they don't drown to lower levels reaching out to drugs for solace.

Reason why kids try out drugs:

1. Peer pressure.
2. To appear cool.
3. Lack of parental supervision.
4. Parents using drugs.
5. Very poor or very rich socio-economic status.
6. Influenced by social media.
7. Influenced by celebrities.
8. Lack of awareness about the deleterious effects of the drugs.
9. Lack of goal in life.
10. Out of boredom.
11. Poor scholastic performance.
12. Domestic violence at home.
13. Broken family.

14. Either parents having extra marital affair.
15. Lack of social and cultural identity.

Protective factors

1. Stable family background.
2. Strong sense of identity.
3. Good scholastic performance.
4. Middle class socio economic status.
5. Having a strong sense of purpose.
6. Having hobbies and involvement in sports.

Addressing the teachers

The teachers should be taught and sensitized about the availability of the various types and forms of drugs. Teachers commonly tend to ridicule and punish the students at large for using drugs. An ideal way to handle the kids would be to ask this question:

"Why are you using drugs?" – this question would be a better ice-breaker and provide a more pragmatic way to approach these kids instead of talking to them with a judgemental tone and label them as "drug users". It is advisable to avoid labelling them as much as possible. It is pertinent to ask this question because each person resorts to using drugs for different reasons. Each of them has a background story and they have a theory on rationalizing their drug use behaviour. It is necessary to understand why the kids are using drugs. Without comprehending their reasons, plain suggestions or preaching on the harmful effects of drugs will not be of any use.

Once the reason for seeking drugs is identified, then we can see what underlying issue needs to be addressed and plan the intervention accordingly.

In the Indian community, it is a common practice to shame a kid in front of his/her peers with the notion that the kid would magically realise and wean off the drugs. On the contrary, this approach will only hasten the addiction process.

School administration

1. The school administration should make mental health services easily accessible to children in need.

2. Can inculcate the practice of token economy (where kids are appreciated by giving them things they like, which in turn will encourage them to exhibit socially desirable behaviours) to kids who are excelling in studies. For example, the class topper can be given a small amount of money so that the child will feel motivated to study hard and retain the topper status; in addition this will also encourage the other kids to perform better as the incentive is alluring.

3. There should be a liaison between the school administration and the nearby psychiatrists who can visit weekly or every fortnightly.

4. Punitive actions must be taken (not in the form of physical or verbal, but small actions like withdrawing the phone, gadgets etc. can be done.)

Note: corporal punishment will definitely backfire and prove counterintuitive.

5. Involvement of parents in the kid's education in the form of conducting parents teachers meetings and ensuring there is at least 80% attendance.

6. Many a time, the school administration tends to ridicule the parents for the wrong doings of the children. This approach will break the harmony in the family and create discord between the parents. It is important to understand the difficulties in the families of each student and empathise with them because everyone we meet is undergoing some form of misery and it would be best if we do not add to the misery and help them instead.

Parents

1. Parenting should be a conscious decision – the children did not ask to be born, it was the parents' decision to have kids. So, it is important to instill in the minds of the parents that they have to take a step to be responsible parents apart from providing clothing and shelter.

2. Parental supervision should be done as far as children's education and access to money is concerned.

3. Parents should know about the children's friends and whom they hang out with most of the time.

4. Children learn from what the parents do rather than from what they preach. What the parents do in front of them will be learnt by the children through modelling. Parents must prove to be ideal role models to their kids.

5. Restricting the amount of pocket money given to children.

6. All said and done, it is also important to "not be too nosy" in the children's affairs.

Police

1. The drug peddlers in all areas should be identified and regulated.

2. Punishments should be given by the book.

3. All juvenile cases should be duly informed to the school authorities and parents.

Intervention to curb drug addiction among school students

Main people to involve in the process:

1. School kids
2. Teachers
3. School administration
4. Parents
5. Police

The commonly used drugs are:

1. Recently "coolip" – a form of tobacco.
2. All forms of cannabis – ganja, hash, bhang etc.

3. <u>LSD stamps</u> – these are initially distributed free of cost to school children to make them addicted, then these stamps are sold at sky high prices. This is an emerging multi-million-dollar business.

4. <u>Other forms of tobacco</u> – cigarettes, beedi, leaves etc. Vaping is a healthier alternative.

5. <u>Alcohol</u> – that is widely available in varied concentrations.

6. <u>Cocaine</u> – common in parties by the rich/affluent as it is costlier. But now its use is becoming more rampant across all social classes.

7. <u>Opioids</u> – these are available as injectables or smoked and snorted as well.

8. <u>Amphetamines</u> – they give a "kick" once inhaled/smoked/ingested. Now they are sold as "strawberry kicks" that come in adorable doll shapes to attract school children.

9. Apart from the above, there are many other drugs that are cropping up under new names, with different combinations of single drugs to give a combined effect.

What is addiction?

I get asked this question many a time. While prescribing medications for their mental health, people are worried that they may get "addicted" to these medicines. In order to explain this, we must first clarify what addiction exactly is. When we say someone is addicted to alcohol what we mean is -

(i)   Their prime aim in life is to drink alcohol.

(ii)   They avoid performing all of their duties and responsibilities.

(iii) Their focus is to seek alcohol, procure alcohol, drink alcohol and repeat.

(iv)   They do not maintain healthy social, work, personal life balance.

(v)   They incur financial losses due to excessive spending to buy booze.

(vi)   They are sometimes in trouble with the law – for breaking rules when under intoxication.

(vii) They have constant disputes or everyday battles with their family members over their addiction as they fail to play their expected roles of father/mother/son/daughter/sister/brother/husband/wife etc.

(viii) They gradually become unable to make a living of their own. They show up to work in a drunk state and get fired or don't go to work at all.

Why are these substances addictive?

The substances that we are concerned about – alcohol, tobacco, cocaine, LSD, cannabis, opioids, solvents, other stimulants, mushrooms etc. when used lead to a direct increase in dopamine level. This dopamine is the hormone responsible for our brains to pick up a certain habit and follow it. For example, the "pleasure" we get when we eat biriyani or ice cream is produced by dopamine. The moment we have a handful of biriyani and transport it to our mouth, the brain sends a dopamine spike. However, this spike is short lived, so the pleasure experienced by the first mouthful of biriyani fades away. This is the reason why "bucket biriyani"s have become famous. The sudden rise in dopamine causes immense pleasure, which results in the brain wanting more and more of it. The downside of this is that the duration of this peak is limited and hence the dopamine surge falls down rapidly. This is why we tend to seek more and more of it. Now, the dopamine rise caused by the substances mentioned in the first line of this paragraph is manifold higher which leads on to higher addictive potential and voracious seeking of that particular substance.

Apart from dopamine surge, these substances also cause a rise in endogenous opioids which beget a sense of euphoria – an extreme sense of artificial happiness and gratitude for this life (the same life that they once despised before using the drug). As it cedes a perception that life is meaningful and temporarily alleviates the pain of everyday chores and mundane activities, the person using it seeks more of the drug as it helps them to tide over their perceived difficult life.

Oxytocin – a hormone that establishes a sense of connection to others is also released at the times of drug usage but this is time limited and tends to fall down drastically the result of which severe addicts turn to themselves and move away from their social circle. You might have heard of alcoholics who used to drink with friends initially, then later as the addiction progressed, they began drinking alone. These lone drinkers are the result of a severe drinking problem which has driven them to lose all their friends because -

(i)   They had picked up fights with their buddies when intoxicated and probably said things they should not have said.

(ii) They had borrowed extensively from their friends to fund their drinking habit and hence their friends have disowned him/her.

(iii) Seeing the addict's unhindered drinking pattern the family members of the addict's friends (usually the wife) have warned them not to hang out with the "addicted friend" fearing their husband might also get influenced. At these situations, the friends who have a more controlled drinking pattern know whom to prioritise in their lives and they would not jeopardize relationship with their significant family members and risk losing them over being friends with someone who has a disrupted behaviour and life.

How to curb addiction?

I have heard many people say, "I can quit drinking even today if I want to".

"நா நினைத்தால் குடியை நிறுத்திவிடுவேன்".

These are usually the people who go on to take de-addiction treatment for a lifetime. In order to come to a conclusion on how to stop this, we should first see how this habit starts.

It all starts with, "Just one sip".

Yes, you read that right. It is always a friend who says, "Just take one sip and all your problems will be solved".

Like I have already discussed before – Prevention is better than Cure. Avoid even taking that first sip. You might have come across some people who proudly declare that they have been drinking for 30 years and nothing has happened to them, so they advocate drinking to their near and dear. They do functionally well and have no signs of addiction. Such people are a lucky few whose brain and body have some mutations, permutations and combinations to metabolize alcohol in a certain way in which none of the bodily functions are hampered.

YOU CAN NEVER GUESS WHAT KIND OF RESPONSE YOUR BODY WILL GIVE TO DURGS.

The best advice from my side for this problem would be:-

"துஷ்டனைக் கண்டால் தூர விலகு".

We should strive to a live a problem free life as much as possible because life is difficult already. We need not make it more complicated by inviting problems. The best life to live is a wise life where we navigate efficiently through problems and spend our precious time and energy on things that really matter instead of seeking treatment for addiction that would not have existed had we said a firm "NO" to the first drink that was offered long long ago.

Another reason why school kids turn to drugs is BOREDOM. They get bored easily and hence it is our duty to invoke the intellect into exploring productive strategies that would nourish the creative potential and add a healthy meaning to life.

How to find the purpose and meaning of one's life?

Many youngsters these days are in search of their unique meaning and purpose for their birth and life. While this search is not that detrimental, the adolescents' undecided ambitions and unfocussed pursuits and lack of availability of a streamlined path to a promising career is a lot detrimental. This wavering mind cultivates an unquenching relentless thirst for exploring and experiencing new ventures and imagining an unforeseeable future.

In other words, most kids are happy living in their own "delulu". I am not the one to discourage imagination and individual opinions. Following one's dream may sound really glamourous and charming. But at what cost?

The first step is to be able to stand first and then practice running. If you are not from a financially secure background, how much of risk can be taken to pursue one's dream? The safe bet would be to attain a financially stable status and then pursue dreams. This thought must be inculcated into young minds from a very young age so they don't get lost into their fantasy world and lose touch with reality. With the humongous opportunities that has arisen with technological revolution, children are actually at loggerheads with their future because no career can guarantee a promising future.

The best we can do is – help our kids select a stream/course that they have at least a little bit of interest in, build skills that can be of use to garner material wealth so we can make a living out of that. If kids happen to have some specific areas of interests or goals, they can be encouraged to build on it later on. If financial need is not a constraint, then they can be encouraged to pursue whatever they want right from a young age.

Also it is monumental to make them understand the definition of success. Some kids are easily carried away by the notion that attaining fame and money is the ultimate aim of life and if they don't attain that niche in society they deem themselves as a failure.

<u>Fame</u>: Being known by people whom you actually don't know. Think about it. Why does it matter? This would extend to other people's opinion of you. Why do you want to bother about some random person's perception of you?

<u>Money</u>: It extends up to infinity and how much money is enough money?

Coming back to finding the purpose of one's life: There is a widespread myth that everyone's life has a purpose. Your life is the same as that of a mosquito. Why would you even think you are better than a mosquito? Each living being has its own functions and abilities. A mosquito can suck blood and inject an anticoagulant into your skin so you don't bleed out and die. Can you do it with your mouth? So, if a mosquito's life has no purpose, then so it is for your life as well. If you are able to live a life of use to yourself and to others, then that it is all there is to it. You have succeeded in life. You have made it.

LIFE IS MEANINGLESS and there is no point is searching for meaning from a meaningless entity. We are traversing this Earth for a limited period of time – roughly about 70-100 years. This is a small fraction of time since the dawn of the BIG BANG. The world is going to spin with or without you in it. If having a purpose and making a change is what you want, then start by loving the people around you and making their lives better. Soon, new pastures will pave way for more abundance and then you can reap the benefits of all the seeds you sowed.

Sex and Relationships

S ex is still a topic of taboo in most areas of Tamilnadu. There are a lot of culture capitalists/guardians (*கலாச்சார காவலர்கள்*) who refrain themselves and those around them from talking about these issues.

What is the need to talk about this?

Adolescence is the phase in our life where our sexual functions develop and attain maturity. Just like we discussed about intellectual part of the brain growing and finding its own area of interest, the sexual part of the brain also seeks stimulus to express itself and explore varied options. Parents and teachers become overwhelmed and dumbstruck when they hear their students or kids have gotten into a romantic relationship with a person of the opposite/same sex. They become thunderstruck if the partner is of the same sex.

There are many elements to discuss here. Let us see one by one.

The urge/desire to talk to a member of the opposite sex

This is a natural biological function and must not be hindered at any cost. The brain forms new connections at this age. This development is necessary for maturation into adult brain and to substantiate healthy adult relationships and for a happy life.

Benefits of encouraging communication with all genders

1. Kids learn that members of the opposite sex have different likes, dislikes, emotions are expressed differently etc.

2. In due course they learn that girls like articulate and verbal communication and that boys prefer shoulder to shoulder type of communication i.e., you can see boys/men bonding easily while watching sports sitting on the couch, whereas girls bond over coffee/tea while facing eye to eye and sharing things from each other's lives.

3. They also learn that everyone irrespective of gender have emotions and experience pain. This is tectonic in preventing all forms of abuse and violence against women/girls. A striking example of this would be the "Pollachi rape cases", where all victims were naïve young girls who were lured into trusting unknown boys/men through text messages and calls. Had only these kids been encouraged into having healthy conversation with each other, these girls would have easily found out the motive behind these calls and would never have ventured into isolated places trusting these "sweet talking" males.

This is evident from the words "நான் உங்களை அண்ணா மாதிரி நினைச்சு தான் பேசினேன், please என்னை விட்டுருங்க அண்ணா", before being brutally raped and video-taped.

What a painful statement!

Healthy communication with the girls would also help the boys understand that girls are just like all other human beings. Boys think that girls are some "exotic" creatures who have no emotions. Something that is unknown to the mind raises curiosity. Hence some boys think of girls as "play toys" and subject them to all their dark sexual fantasies.

4. Knowing how to communicate with members of the opposite sex will pave a long way in living a safe and meaningful life. Most of us want a life where we have people who like us for who we are and not for the sexual favours that they are expecting of us. The more choosy we become in selecting people who have access to our time and energy, more purposeful and fulfilling our life becomes. We become experts in reading people and their intentions only by real life experiences and it does not come from ignoring one gender of the species altogether.

5. We judge people whom we don't know personally. For example, we tend to pass random comments on the lives of celebrities, we like them or don't like them for the reasons that we think are legitimate. This stems from an underlying "Fear of

the Unknown", which is a pronounced trait of the primitive animal brain. In ancient times, when we were hunter gatherers we feared new clans because of the worry that they might hunt us and kill us all – this was a time when speech and language was not as developed as it is today. Fast forward to 2025, we have enough skills to think, speak and communicate. This "Fear of the Unknown" shows up noisily in the ignorant mind when we see people who are quite different from us.

For example, we have many genders that are medically classified with different sexual orientations. First we must have a clear understanding on what is gender and sexual orientation.

(i) <u>Gender</u> – The sense of being "male", "female", "both", "trans-man/woman", etc. There are many genders that people identify with and this must be a matter of personal choice. This must be respected by everyone around them and should not be ridiculed. Strict laws must be enforced to punish people/parents/ teachers who shame kids for their choice on gender identity.

The main problem (perceived by the parents) arises when a child assigned a male gender at birth – during adolescence tends to display characteristics of the female gender or vice versa. The male to female transition is disgusted upon more than the female to male as the parents worry losing their "precious" male child.

Is this a problem?

It is neither a mental nor a physical health problem. This is the way their brain is patterned to develop. It is not something they acquired due to the technological prowess and access to social media or TikTok. This is the way their brain was meant to develop. It is purely genetic. There is no one to blame for this. It is not because of the food the mother ate, or the videos that your child saw.

How painful it is for the child?

You will never understand this struggle until you face it yourself or until you develop excellent empathetic skills where you ask them about their difficulties with the aim of grasping their emotions.

Once a 13 year old boy was brought to my clinic by his wailing mother whose whole world was turned upside down since her "Son" started behaving like a girl and she was desperate to give a medicine to "change" him back to "normal". Like I have explained before, this is not an illness to change. It is just the way they are. To be more specific, their brain is destined to develop these traits even while inside the uterus. There is nothing you can do to change it and I can't emphasize this enough – this is not an abnormality to be changed.

When I spoke to the boy, he said, "Doctor, it is very difficult for me. I hate wearing these boy clothes. I want to wear churidhar, bangles and grow my hair. My body is female but my parents are not understanding. I feel disgusted to be touched by boys. And everyone mistakes me when I sit next to girls but I am most comfortable only around them". His exact words, *"பசங்க பக்கத்துல உக்காந்தா எனக்கு கூச்சமா இருக்கு"*, still lingers in my mind.

This is a child whose feelings are not validated by the society he lives in and his parents/ extended family members trying their best to make him lead a usual life just like everyone else. The main reason why parents view this concept as alien and derogatory to their standard of living is because of the rights of the transgenders and their lives. Most of them are chased away by their family members because they want to uphold their imaginary "Privilege". They dread upon the opinions of their friends and family who are actually worried about their own lives and this is the least of their concerns.

Another reason is that once they are chased away, such kids turn to begging and take up painful jobs as commercial sex workers because without education it is difficult to survive in this dog eat dog world. With this in the background, the general population has a negative opinion on transgenders as they see them begging on the roads. This is a sad portrayal of them in the Indian society and again, stringent laws must be enforced to ensure their safety.

Here, I would like to thank our ex chief minister Mr. Karunanidhi who has given the name *"திருநங்கை"* to such people thereby creating a respectable identity for them and equal opportunities.

Despite all measures, more awareness needs to be raised in the society to accept everyone regardless of who they are or what they like. Now, we also have certain jobs that are acceptive of transgenders and we can even see transgenders in socially respectable positions. Still a long way to go!

The boy who came to my clinic, did not show up after 3 sessions. As I write this, I sincerely hope he is somewhere living his best life and is in safe hands.

(ii) <u>Sexual orientation:</u> This is the gender or genders to which you are romantically and sexually attracted to. For example, if you are a male and attracted to a female – you are said to be Heterosexual. If you are a male and attracted to a male, you are said to be Homosexual. In other words, being attracted to members of a different sex is heterosexual. Most of the general population are heterosexuals. Being attracted to members of the same sex is called being "Homosexual". Colloquially men attracted to men are called Gay. Women attracted to women are called Lesbian. There are some people who are attracted to members of both the sex called "Bisexual". There are many other types of sexual orientation but for the purposes of this book, let us stick to these alone. Heterosexuality is widely, socially and legally accepted. So there is not much to talk about it. What comes off as a thunderstorm to Indian parents is when their kids come out of the closet and open up to them that they are gay/lesbian etc. This is not a matter of life and death. Like I have mentioned the cause of gender identity, the concept of sexual orientation is also genetically determined to a certain extent and it is largely a personal choice. There is no right/wrong about this. It is not something that you should or should not approve of.

If you do not understand "Why", then it is high time you seek knowledge and read the science behind this and not give arbitrary comments belittling other people's choices.

Do's and Don'ts regarding adolescent romantic relationships

1. The first reflex that comes when we see our teen in a romantic relationship is – take away the phone, cut down all access to gadgets, follow their activities etc. This is definite "NO". It must not be done at any cost. When you try to break their relationship, it will only get stronger. The teenage years are when they will do exactly what they are told not to do. And will do the exact opposite of what they are told to do. The stronger you oppose, stronger will be their need to continue the relationship.

The best thing you can do is enquire them excitedly about who their partner is, how did they meet, what they like about them etc. This will help you maintain a healthy relationship with your teen. Once you gain their confidence, they will feel like sharing everything with you. Instead of panicking, tell your teen to invite their partner over to your house for tea or dinner.

The best part of today's teen relationships is in due course, they themselves will grow apart and break up. It is just a matter of time. Also in order to regulate their daily routine, we can make a "deal" with them saying that they can have a lunch date with their partner if they score high marks in the oncoming exams. This is to keep them oriented to their reality so they don't get lost in their romantic fantasies. Because the first love is always the most exciting and thrilling one! Let them enjoy that while also being functional.

It is noxious to the parents if the romantic partner chosen by their child is a useless loafer on the streets. We cannot hide our emotional fire from surfacing up seeing our child getting infatuated to a lowlife. But it is momentous to maintain our calm while dealing with such baneful situations at home. The reason why some girls tend to be attracted to such boys is because these boys take tremendous efforts to look "Cool". The tattoos, pierced eyebrows etc. seem appealing to the eyes who have only seen well combed, oiled hair and boring student lifestyles. I don't intend to convey that having tattoos and piercings is wrong! It is their individual choice and needs to be respected. I used these examples to explain that we are always attracted to what is lacking in us. For example, the Indian/south Indian men find girls who have a lighter skin tone attractive because melanin is abundant in the south Indian skin and we naturally have a darker skin tone, hence the white skin is seen as "beautiful" and becomes the most sought after in the marriage market.

To be honest, even I was attracted to a drug addict at one point in my life. All this is part of natural evolution where we find the "different" to be fascinating. If such girls are encouraged to also study side by side and pursue a career, they will soon grow out of this phase and seek worthy life partners. It may not be an easy task from the parents' side, for help please seek professional assistance.

Other relationships

Friendship: Adolescence is the period in life where kids slowly grow away from their parents and pine to create a separate identity for themselves. They have an innate biological mechanism that propels them to seek people and friends who are not similar to their family because nature knows that breeding within the same family will lead to genetically weak offsprings and this is nature's way of protecting the human race. Some families have ancestral ethics where they marry within the same families in which case nature loses its potency shielding them and succumbs to acquired relationships thereby producing kids with a wide range of disabilities including physical and mental illnesses.

These adolescent relationships are vital to the developing brain as it enhances a sense of connection and induces a sense of belongingness to the larger group. This notion of "being part of a larger group" perpetuates the feeling of security, which is protective against suicidal tendencies. Apart from this, the morals that they learnt during their childhood from their parents are all put to test and re-organised depending on their current social circle. If they have a habit of reading intellectually stimulating books, they will begin to discuss what they read and debate on what is right and wrong. If they tend to use drugs or drink and smoke as a group, then they will soon be tempted to experience other self-destructive and anti-social activities including sexual harassment (not in the near future but may happen at any point in life, the seeds of which are planted in adolescence). As parents and teachers we cannot curate every second of our children's life and decide whom they can and cannot be friends with.

As goes the popular Thamizh saying,

"மாட்டுக்கு தண்ணியை காட்டத்தான் முடியும்", which in English means – a cow can only be shown water, we cannot make a cow drink it.

So sit back and relax. We are all doing our best to make our children happy and healthy. We do not control the entire outcome. What we have is an illusion of control. If your child strays around a lot creating distress in you, we can try therapy. But many a times, we cannot help someone who does want to be helped. Maybe it is a curse of this generation to see our offsprings drown in deep waters while we remain helpless! But with that being said, we can always try! A dream and a little hope can create revolutions.

How to ensure our kids have the right friends?

This is the constant worry of the Indian parent. You can start by teaching them to become the right friend. Teach them values. It starts by initiating and maintaining healthy communication with your child. This goes back to their toddler period. You cannot afford to ignore their childhood and jump right back into their teen phase with the motive of becoming their "buddy". Kids are smarter than you can imagine and they will sense your intentions from afar. So the best bet is to uphold a secure and a certain relationship with them.

If you had missed out on their childhood phase but you are willing to take up the parenting role in adolescence:

This used to be common 10-20 years ago when parents traded their time for money and hence were not able to be there for their children. This is not a crime because we all grow up in different family situations and have different priorities as we age. I would rather say that we cannot hold children as collateral damage to our own dreams and fantasies. It is good that you have taken the step now to make amends.

The first step would be – Be honest with your intentions. Surrender instead of building guilt inducing stories.

For example, **don't** say, "I have sacrificed a lot for you, I was working so you can have food on your plate and go to the best school in town".

Instead say, "I am sorry I have missed out on a lot of your childhood days, I thought I was doing what was best but it looks like things are not how I thought it would turn out to be. I am ready to change myself and be a better parent for you, please give me a chance".

Children these days, prefer overt communication to hidden agendas. If it works it works, if it doesn't it doesn't. Again don't beat yourself up much about this second innings. If they don't realise it now, they will probably realise it when they become parents themselves just like me. We all have only one shot at life. Life is too precious for you to keep worrying about what you could've done differently. Your past no longer exists. It is only a story in your mind. You have the power in you to change the same old depressing story you keep telling yourself. Your child will understand your life once he/she grows old and begets a child themselves. All your attempts, advices, sacrifices will start to make sense and a gush of forgiveness and gratitude will ebb in them as they slowly let go off all the contempt and rage they had inside them. After all you were just doing your best. And your love was abundant. You did what you knew and what you could at that time. Don't wait for your child to forgive you. Forgive yourself and just let go. This letting go is invaluable for you to live your life in peace.

Mentorship/Well-wisher

It is common for teens to derail from mainstream academic and social life and drift to become the outliers of the society where they get devoured into socially undesirable behaviours leading a life that is doomed to perish. Given this bearish nature and the fickle mindedness that accompanies adolescence it would massively help having a mentor or a well-wisher whom our kids can confide in and look up to. This mentor can even be the child's mother or father, an uncle or an aunt... or a poet from ancient Thamizh literature, for example, I feel more connected to poet subramaniya Bharathi than towards anybody else who lives or has lived on this planet. Mentors and soulmates can come in many ways, shapes or forms. Children should be given ample opportunities to explore all of this – the first step is to introduce them to a library.

It is up to the child to decide who they would turn up to for answers to their unending questions. Seldom do teens look up to their parents as their biology tells them to view parents as potential threat and that they should move away from them as much as they can. In order for kids to get hold on to a right mentor, they should first know about the different kinds of people in the world. Reading is the only medium to attain this. In today's age, reading is replaced to a certain extent by podcasts – which are albeit a good alternative to reading.

Reading can help forage into all the brilliant minds that exist and have existed and directly teleport you to a whole new different world.

What parents cannot do at certain crucial times in the life of a teen can be done by a mentor.

Psychosis

Let me make certain things clear before I proceed to explain psychosis. We have come across this term called "psycho" which is often used colloquially in a derogatory manner to insult someone who behaves in a way which we don't generally appreciate. The term "psycho" is derived from the Greek word "psyche" which literally means the mind. So, when someone calls another person a "psycho" it does not mean anything language wise because that word does not convey insult in its own sense. What this conveys on the other hand is the illiterate nature of the mind of the person using this word. It is highly recommended to refrain from using this word in an inappropriate manner.

Psychosis is a clinical condition in which the person hears voices of someone talking to them when nobody else is around. This (auditory hallucination) is a common symptom. Studies have shown that when a person hallucinates the same areas of brain that would be activated when a "normal" person hears would be activated in a hallucinating individual. This implies that hallucination is a real experience and not a figment of one's imagination.

They feel that everyone around them is talking ill about them and are conspiring against them to harm them. These feelings are very real for the person undergoing this tremendous invisible pain and suffering and it will not help them if you keep telling them "It is all in your head". Nobody would choose to suffer. Because of this underlying agony, they don't communicate as much to those around them, they don't feel like eating or sleeping, sometimes even taking a bath becomes difficult. Such people find it difficult to comprehend what is happening in their surroundings and they appear confused and muddled up in their own thoughts. They may sometimes talk irrelevantly and make no sense.

All this is due to an imbalance in the dopamine pathway in the brain. It is not an issue that you can talk this person out of nor a possession by a ghost which you can exorcise. This is a clinical mental health condition which needs immediate psychiatric help. It is completely manageable and such people can go on to lead happy fulfilling lives. Psychosis is not a condition that is incompatible with human life. If you know anyone suffering from such symptoms kindly educate them about the nature of the illness and encourage them to seek professional help.

Seizures

This is also called as "Fits". In classical common cases it is seen as abnormal involuntary movements of limbs and body, accompanied mostly but not always by tongue bite, up rolling of eyes, involuntary passing of motion and/or urine. There are many types of seizures that go undiagnosed until very late thereby postponing treatment efficacy and adding burden to the person's life. I don't want to discuss in detail about all the different types and its neural basis. I will share the symptoms that should prompt us to consult a specialist.

1. Falling down often without reason despite having adequate balance.
2. Lip smacking, frequent blinking.
3. Suddenly dropping to the floor and not trying to get up immediately because of loss of consciousness.
4. Repeating certain hand gestures or bodily movements and staying unresponsive to external conversations during these episodes.
5. Suddenly folding hands in front of the chest as in saying "vanakkam", (வணக்கம்).
6. Frequent episodes when they are spontaneously talking about a particular topic that is not connected to them in any way, and then having no recollection of what happened.

7. Vacant stare without being oriented to the surroundings.

8. Apart from this, if there is any other behaviour that your child exhibits that is of concern to you, please seek professional help.

Conversion Disorder

This is a type of mental health issue which manifests itself as abnormal movements of limbs and hence it is misconceived as seizure. These symptoms are classically characterised by throwing movements of limbs, thrusting movements of the hip, tightly closed eyes being resistant to opening as opposed to up rolling of eyes in real seizures, no involuntary voiding of urine or motion, sudden falls where they land safely most of the time without sustaining major injuries.

Sometimes when people are not able to vocalise their psychological stress or handle and communicate their mental stresses in a safe manner, they SUBCONSCIOUSLY tend to **Convert** their mental agony into physical symptoms. This is not a conscious mechanism which confirms that these people are not "acting" and are not deliberately doing it. You will not be able to help them if you keep telling them that they can control it if they can. The reason for this stems from not providing a safe confidential warm space for these kids to talk and deliver their emotions, feelings.

This is more common in women from lower socio-economic living situations where they are largely undermined, not respected, don't have a job, cannot be financially independent, – all these point to a situation where their emotional concerns are not even considered and hence they **"Convert"** as the stress is insurmountable and they do not have any other let out mechanism.

Among adolescents, studies have shown that this is commoner in girls than in boys. The reason being the same as described above. Once these symptoms start showing up – these kids are attended to, given importance, and are relieved from going to school, all their needs are met and are given princess treatment. This results in what we call **"Secondary Gain"** – a gain in means of emotional well-being where there is temporary alleviation of symptoms due to the excess attention and needs being met. If this "extra attention" continues to grow, the child will never get better. This **Secondary Gain** maintains the illness as opposed to help curing it.

The cause of this set of symptoms (the conversion disorder) is an underlying cry for help where the child's emotional needs are not met. When the emotional needs are met in the form of **"Secondary Gain"**, the converting symptoms will become stronger because if the symptoms fade away, the secondary gain (attention from care-givers) is also going to fade away. So the child will have a tendency to convert again and again to get the **"Secondary Gain"** from his/her family members. The symptoms will start to surface up.

How to deal with these kids so their propensity to **convert** decreases?

1. Acknowledge their distress.
2. Before diagnosing it yourself, please seek expert opinion and follow their advice. Understand that the treating doctors are experts in their chosen fields and they can help you understand the illness maintaining factors and causing factors.
3. Even though it is a converting mechanism, their suffering is real to them.
4. Treat the child as normal as possible. They should not be given any special attention.
5. There should not be any exemption from performing their regular duties like going to school or washing their plates after eating.
6. No additional vacations or gifts unnecessarily.
7. All the people living in the house with the child must attend family therapy sessions because the parenting style affects the intellectual and emotional development of the child and any discrepancies among the family members' reaction to the converting symptoms may play havoc with the emotional maturation of the child's developing brain.
8. Medications are helpful in severe cases but this must be decided by the treating psychiatrist and not by the family members.

Technology and Social Media

With the rise in the advent of new technologies and rise in the engagement of the general population on the internet, the world has literally come into every person's hands. We now have the ability to be digitally present anywhere in the world and even in other planets (provided Elon Musk's generosity) all the while physically staying in our own rooms. Is this a boon or a bane? Every invention/discovery till date has never been proven absolutely useless or useful, it all has its own merits and demerits. Even a useless invention has been turned to be useful by being a subject of debate provoking minds to ponder over it hence proving to be of some benefit.

Internet has been a unifying factor promoting globalistion curbing the social divide between the rich and the poor. By "**Social divide**", I mean internet has provided everyone with access to any kind of information and resources at an era when "**Information was equivalent to Wealth**".

Now, the notion has changed where we equate "**Freedom of time as Wealth**". The ability to do whatever we want to do and be wherever we want to be is considered wealth and is adorned by one and all. More than promoting contentment, it is being "fancied" upon, and has now lead to increased envy and dissatisfaction with life owing to the constant comparison of one's personal life with everyone else's positive highlight reel on social media. This leads to a pursuit of happiness which would seem elusive and finally people are just left to deal alone with their perceived miserable lives.

Knowledge and education

This is a big plus of the internet. For example, our very own Mr. Gukesh has become the world's youngest chess champion and Indians all over the world are rejoicing. This was made possible because of the connectedness provided by internet. Also, this has increased attention towards chess and kids may start asking, "What is chess? Can I too learn chess?" It is when kids ask these kinds of questions we know that we are raising our kids right.

Many competitive exams (not talking about NEET) conducted across the world are being known by students in every part of the world which helps them achieve their dreams. Study materials and mock tests are conducted online by trusted institutions which help them ascend quicker to glory.

The downside of it

This widespread access to people across the world has prompted the narcissists and people with psychopathic tendencies to prey upon naïve vulnerable kids and sometimes adults threatening them to pay money or laundering it through other carefully structured own fool proof protocols. They have unique algorithms which target aimless teens and youngsters promising them with an astonishing future provided they obey everything they are asked to do and click on every link they are sent. It is not healthy being paranoid all the time and suspecting every internet friend your child has. Having pen pals can foster intellectual growth and enrich one's life with platonic relationships. These kinds of relationships have a pinch of magic in them that can never be felt with others. The thrill of talking to someone who lives a life that is a lot different from one's own life can enhance one's perception of the world and generate a feeling of inclusivity, re-inforcing Kaniyan Poongunranaar's -

"யாதும் ஊரே யாவரும் கேளிர்".

We cannot guess what kind of friends our kids will find on the internet. There are a lot of applications that lock certain websites that are risky to children. We can **Reduce Harm** by installing such software and let nature take its own course.

It is not advisable to pry on our child's internet use. We can have casual discussions with them while cooking or doing the laundry which will leave them off guard and let them open up about their private life if they feel warm and comfortable around us.

If they find a hint of suspicion in our tone, then all our efforts will prove futile thereby hindering all our future attempts to understand them. In Thamizh, I would describe handling adolescents as handling,

"கன்னிவெடி", one wrong step and you are doomed forever.

Doom scrolling

A lot on why this is happening has been described previously. Adding on to that, this will steal you off your precious time. Time is considered to be the only precious moiety of all human possessions, because you can never get it back once lost and you cannot buy in excess. Everything else is replaceable.

To begin with, we can attempt to create awareness in them by proposing to play a game where each of us can scroll for 2 minutes straight and then recall what we have scrolled. During this recall, there is an 87% chance that they cannot recall more than 3-4 feeds, among those 3-4 are the ones they have last seen.

This is because their short term memory is impaired, hence the first few items are not remembered; the feeds retained through the visual modality are retained for a few seconds and are recalled albeit easily. The hippocampal cells are slowly degenerating and if left unchecked it will start showing up in personality and soon the brain will not be able to handle life and will eventually grow to become dependent upon another being for survival. Who was once an active vibrant person would grow up to become a slow laid back person because of the long standing under performance of the hippocampal cells due to under-usage; (not implying that a slow laid back life is not good, the point of focus here is the **change** of potential and how we suit our needs for life based on the functioning of our brain).

In other words, we all have heard of kids who were outstanding scholars in primary school but after middle school their performance had deteriorated and they are no longer their younger selves with full potential.

Scoring marks is not the only yardstick to measure the potential of one's brain but given our current academic structure it is indeed the only yardstick and it pains me writing this sentence.

A lot has been discussed in various forums on "restricted screen time" for kids and it is a number game with some studies saying one hour per day, while some saying 30 minutes would suffice. Not all educational resource is available in a "book" format and most of the latest research is immediately accessible only through the internet. It would be a crime to not let kids have access to internet. What can possibly be done? If there is a genuine requirement of a smart phone or laptop and if it exceeds the said time, then it is agreeable to let them use it until their need is met. This can be achieved by maintaining a healthy communication with your child and actively involving in their problems and academics not with a view of "spying" but with a view of "understanding" and making the whole process enjoyable. It should be like your final year group project that you worked on with your friends. Ring a bell?? Yes, that is exactly what I am talking about.

Apart from this, we should follow the basic harm reduction strategies like using those special glasses (which are widely available – please get a standard one and don't be fooled by the cheap fancy ones) to cut down blue light, reduce screen brightness, avoid using phone in a dark room, frequent walks and breaks in between so they don't become sedentary etc.

Another important tip here is the introduction of books to children from as early as 3-4 years will create a good addiction in their brain to the paraphernalia of reading, wherein they find pleasure in buying a book, excitedly anticipating the arrival of a book, opening it, seeing the cover, the size, the smell of the pages, make a mental plan on how many pages they would want to read per day, be oriented to the book as they read (which is absent while reading an e-book) because they will be seeing and feeling the number of pages they have already read (which gives them a feeling of accomplishment due to a natural healthy rise of dopamine in the brain) and the bulk of pages they are yet to read and gain knowledge from (this anticipatory excitement promotes the intellectualization of the brain which would prevent them from derailing into unhealthy addictions and activities).

The more you know, the more you want to know!

If you can obtain pleasure from reading, then you can withstand any obstacle that life throws at you. It is a good drug to become addicted to and the feeling of "High" a good book gives you is more pleasurable than cocaine. Finding that "Good Book" that can engage you in a deep conversation is a challenge though! Reading is pertinent not only for kids but also for adults.

Suicide

World health organization defines suicide as "the act of deliberately killing oneself". This is considered a social and mental health issue.

Why is it a mental health issue?

The brain of all living beings including that of a unicellular amoeba, has the innate mechanism of procreation and protecting oneself from all sorts of danger. When a lion chases you, you run. At this point when your life is in danger, you don't stop to analyse –

   (i)   Is it socially appropriate to run?
   (ii)   What will others think of me?
   (iii)   Is my boss around?
   (iv)   If you are a mother with your child, you will ensure your child is free from danger and wil not care about anyone else around you.

This act of resorting to any level to protect one's life is a basic instinct and is characteristic of a healthy mind. When the brain is basically programmed to live and procreate and if it suddenly functions in a way in which it makes someone want to end their life, it should be considered as a "Bug" in the system akin to a virus in your software. This problem in the brain manifests itself as a mental illness and hence must be treated.

Postmortem studies on brains of people who died by committing suicide showed that there was a change in the concentration of the "5HTT" receptors indicating that the thoughts of suicide is the result of an underlying abnormality in the way the brain handles serotonin proving that prompt treatment would have prevented the individual from committing suicide. So, if you hear anyone talk about how worthless life is or they'd rather be dead, please take their words seriously and intervene. By intervention I mean, don't give them life advice but take them to a nearby therapist and also inform their first emergency contact to ensure their safety. This small step would go a long way in detailing their life.

Causes of suicide among school children

20 years ago, the reasons of completed suicide were mostly due to an undiagnosed mental illness. Lately, we are seeing a rise in the number of children and adolescents wanting to end their life. When reason for this is probed, they reveal that they don't want to die, but they just want to relieve themselves of the overwhelming mental pain and agony by deliberately harming themselves. This is evident by the cut marks seen mostly in their wrists, forearm, inner thighs etc. This is commoner in girls than in boys – for genetic and hormonal reasons – a reason which we cannot hold them responsible for because harming the self through inflicting pain releases "endogenous opioids" that provide a sense of relief from all sorts of pain including mental and physical.

Opioids are substances that have excellent pain relieving properties and are used following surgeries to reduce pain. It is also used in cancer patients who are not able to tolerate pain. Opioids are released naturally by the body to cut down the effects of pain producing substance.

That is why some kids resort to hurting themselves. There is a misconception that people self-harm with the sole intention of gaining attention from family members and their girlfriends or boyfriends. This may be a secondary gain but the not the sole reason. Such people experience enormous amounts of pain building up within themselves causing excess pressure.

Imagine a pressure cooker with rice in it – it has been cooking for a while, all the water has been used, the pressure inside it rises and rises – if the pressure is let out, we can salvage the cooker and the rice, if we don't let out the pressure we might end up losing both the cooker and the rice. The same happens in the minds of people harming themselves. If they don't release the pressure, they might turn detrimental to themselves and to others. Hence, they cut and let the opioids rush in to alleviate the trauma and as a side effect – the mental pain is also alleviated. They turn to this behaviors time and again because they have not been taught how to deal with overpowering emotions and to express them healthily.

Some kids turn to **"Tattoo Parlors"** so they don't end up hurting themselves but get the same benefit because the underlying need is to inflict pain. Getting a tattoo is a different need and it should not be used for these purposes because this does not address the underlying problem and only perpetuates it. Life is difficult and there are going to be novel problems arising out of thin air as days go by – if we are going to get a tattoo for every problem, then one body wouldn't suffice. I have seen many young people regret the tattoos they got out of an emotional outburst and spend a fortune to get it removed.

How can we deal with kids/adults who turn to harming themselves?

My first treatment for any such act – exercise, exercise, exercise. If it still doesn't get better, consult a nearby therapist but I am sure such symptoms will improve by 70-80% with exercise alone.

In addition to that, encourage them to journal their distressing thoughts –

(i) With time/date,

(ii) Incident which provoked it,

(iii) Their reaction to it,

(iv) Consequence of their reaction,

(v) The way they felt at that time,

(vi) The foods they ate,

(vii) Bowel habit,

(viii) Menstrual cycle co-relation with the date (if female),

— would help them develop emotional intelligence over their symptoms and overcome this behaviour efficiently and permanently.

Why is it a social concern?

The judiciary system in most countries is painstakingly drafted to ensure the safety and security of the rich at the cost of imposing stringent laws on the common people like you and me. We are all aware of the billionaire businessmen whose loans were waivered in a jiffy while the poorest of the poor farmers with 5-10 lakhs loans were made to kill themselves.

You cannot be expected to be happy and healthy when you are surrounded by people who belittle your opinions and thoughts, unless you are rich or in power.

That being said, we should strive to build a mentally healthy society. Most of our happiness is lost in maintaining an imaginary "honor" – கௌரவம்.

This exists only in your minds and nobody else has the time or energy to analyse your life and assess how honorable you are. This is one of the reasons for committing suicide in the Thamizh society – what if the others come to know of our debt? They (the bank people who have abused them while coming to collect debt money) have insulted me using swear words in front of everyone, how will I face my neighbors?

"நீ என்ன வேணா நெனச்சுக்கோ... எனக்கு என்ன?"

This mindset will help you live a life of freedom and with freedom comes enormous responsibility – the responsibility of becoming the happiest and the best version of yourself!

Why do some people want to die?

When the people who survived their suicidal attempts were interviewed on why they wanted to die, 95% of them gave the same answer. They needed an escape from their current life situation. They wanted to live a life that was entirely different from what they were living and they never saw any hope of their dreams coming true one day. They were not fed up with life itself but just fed up with the one they were living.

In order to manifest your dreams, you have to be a little delusional. Have a strong belief in something that no one else can foresee or agree to. And stay delusional while silently working towards it – this unearths the magic that everyone awaits to happen for them. The secret is – Survive the boring days where you have to do the same thing over and over again. But even during this hustle, there is the joy of seeing a yellow butterfly or the miracle of witnessing a pink sky on a rainy evening. It is these small things that add beauty and value to your everyday life. Watching fireworks **everyday** would make you hate it.

I don't promise everyone that everything is a possibility, but we can definitely try! If we fail, we can proudly say, "At least I tried!"

Suicide has been ascribed to an act of valor. For example, I remember studying in school, there was a freedom fighter named Irumporai who refused to eat the food given to him in jail because it was kicked by the jailer and finally died of starvation. This was portrayed as a heroic act as the protagonist prioritized his self-respect to hunger and rather died than eating that meal.

I always say people should treat everyone with respect irrespective of caste, creed, post, cadre, financial status, gender, physical appearance, color etc.

In this context, if I am in jail and ill-treated, the first need is to survive. No matter what. The ideal set of actions would be – eat the meal, survive, remember his name and face, get released from jail, then take action. If we want to create an impact, we should be in positions of power lest all our efforts and screams will go in vain. Gaining freedom is the cumulative result of the actions of millions of people across India, and if I have to regulate everyone's actions and behaviour, the first requirement is to be alive!

Likewise, if social media glorifies certain suicidal deaths that occurred as a result of social injustice, there are going to be more deaths. This is called "copycat suicide". If there is a pressing social issue, unfortunately it takes time – sometimes decades and centuries to correct it and we should have the perseverance and determination to pursue and attain it. Justice and independence cannot be sought overnight unless millions of dollars are at stake!

In this era, we need to be exceedingly tolerant while also working to ameliorate the inequalities. For the brain to be more tolerant, we should reduce the action of the amygdala (the emotional brain), so we can rope in the pre-frontal cortex (the thinking brain) to make more rational safe decisions that would prove beneficial in the long run. The amygdala is the reason for our rage following the news of rapes and murders, we talk about it for a week and then forget. We should use the pre-frontal cortex to analyse, study, discover patterns and then implement strategies to prevent them. Sudden emotional outburst will not solve anything and has no purpose than to make the current situation a bit dramatic and provide topics to discuss over coffee for a few days.

Hobbies and the Importance of
"சும்மா இருத்தல்"

Many parents want their kids to ascend the academic and social ladder saving "years" so they can be ahead of the rest of the cohort.

My question to them is, "What is the point of this haste?"

By instilling the mindset of "I have to be ahead of the others" in kids, we are subconsciously teaching them that they have to compare themselves with their peers constantly, which in turn makes the mind satiated only through external validation. This is a potential threat to developing "happiness" which entirely depends upon internal validation.

Whenever a child expresses interest in something, we naturally tend to enroll them in a class that attempts to expose more of this and nurture it in a structured way so they develop expertise in that field. For example, if a child loves to kick things, we might want to send him/her to a football class.

What I would suggest is – give them more time at figuring out the functions of a few more areas of their brain that may have more potential in one field than the other.

<u>Implication</u> – a child who loves kicking things around can be sent to a football teaching class, but not immediately – give it 2-3 months' time. If it persists, then we can think on proceeding further with this. Children develop a myriad of interest that are fleeting. This is part of natural childhood.

<u>Parents' plight</u> – the moment they enroll their child in a football class, they soon imagine a future where their child is the next Ronaldo. This is not wrong; but when children are expected to fulfill a dream of achieving a Himalayan task, the same act which was once a source of joy, becomes a burden and excruciating to them.

Here we should understand the importance of having a hobby. For everyone (including children and adults) a hobby is a stress relieving act. Hobbies should be seen as fulfilling that sole purpose and nothing else; if you are able to monetise from your hobby, then it is to be considered a "bonus". Hobbies cause the mind to relax naturally and if you have a hobby that you enjoy, then that alone will protect you from many mental and physical illnesses by reducing inflammation in the mind-body circuit. Studies have shown when people who were actively (atleast 4 hours a week) involved in any hobby (majority of the people included in the study had hobbies of painting, playing the piano, playing soccer, cooking with their partner, yoga) had reduced levels of inflammatory markers. This means they are also protected from developing depression, hypertension, diabetes and heart attack compared to similar age people with no hobbies.

Hobbies if developed and encouraged since childhood, have a profound effect on the developing brains which also enhance creativity. This creativity is largely under-estimated in our population where we are taught by our "moral policing adults" that "asking questions" is a symptom of arrogance.

When a mind has a large creative resource, that mind can see the world more beautiful than the rest of the ordinary non-creative minds. This enhances the perception which in turn leads to more inventions and discoveries. This may be one of the reasons why India has not promoted much to the scientific development in the last 2000 years as opposed to living with perfectly designed drainage systems which was lacking everywhere else in this world 5000-10,000 years ago.

This creativity can also produce happiness hormones – serotonin, dopamine and oxytocin thereby helping us build a strong stable healthy well-connected society.

It has been common among parents to discuss – "What class they are sending their children to on weekends".

We need not make every second count – by calculating every minute of their day and engaging them in some class or the other. Being productive and being occupied are two entirely different things.

What is being productive?

Mindfully engaging in any activity – it could be organizing the kitchen drawers, mowing the lawn, having a chat with friends and family, or going to any class which results in self-perceived relaxation and not socially approved relaxation, the list is endless. You can also be productive by doing absolutely nothing. Yes! You can sit still staring into thin air for hours together. You can even spend the weekend completely bored out of your head. That's absolutely fine! Everything you do in life need not have a quantifiable outcome. We can do things just for the heck of it. You can even do laundry while jamming to your favorite song. This gives more happiness than that late night party you had wrecking your sleep and gut.

What is being occupied/busy?

Being busy and occupied have become status symbols which we proudly advertise but we seldom say "I did nothing" with pride. This is mindlessly doing activities that we don't really like or appreciate and don't value – which actually leads to an increase in stress levels. If you like and enjoy the activities that you are occupied with, this raises "your perceived meaning and purpose in life" which makes you want to live longer. But running from one errand to another just to be a socially accepted "busy person" will not be fruitful.

There is something called **"Intuitive Learning"** in Psychiatry. An experiment was conducted with a gorilla locked inside a cage and a banana was kept outside the cage. There was also a stick that was kept outside the cage, at a distance which was within the gorilla's arm distance, while the banana was outside the arm's reach. The gorilla tried to reach the banana many times with its arms, but, failed as it was quite far from its reach. It kept on trying again and again; after many failed attempts it gave up. It was not attempting and was just sitting still.

Then suddenly, the gorilla reached out for the stick, took it and used the stick to slide the banana inside the cage and enjoyed the ripe banana happily. This is called **Intuitive Learning**. The factors to consider here are:

1. There was no teaching on how to use the stick.
2. There were no trials made by the gorilla using the stick.
3. The idea of using the stick just "came" – like a spark.
4. It came after a period of "giving up" and remaining idle.

Human examples would be – Isaac Newton who discovered gravity after an apple fell on his head when he was sitting idly under it. He might have been solving equations in his mind but nobody really knows. The fact that he was sitting under a tree in the daytime points more in favor of "he was just trying to relax".

By these above-mentioned examples, I would like to convey the importance of doing "Nothing" from time to time. Being idle all the time, is definitely not advisable but we all need some time to unwind, where the brain architecture rewires itself so it can gain new functions.

Another life lesson to be learnt from "Intuitive Learning" is – life does not end after you have given up. Maybe something new and unexpected will pop up. We are all human beings employed by our emotions. It is common to finally say, "I have had enough of this", when we are stuck at a point in life where we can never see the light. It is natural to want to let go of things that we are tightly holding on to. And it is not a crime to let go. That's alright. Once you let go, in a few days or months, your mind will come up with something miraculous that can easily solve that pending issue. Trust in your mind.

In order to build a mind that you can trust, the mind must be fertilized with all the necessary nutrition, exercise, people etc. that I have described throughout this book. For more details about the mind – there is a chapter "What is the Mind and Where is it?" in my previous book "Buy Happiness from a Bookshelf" available on Amazon.

MISCELLANEOUS

Especially for Teachers – How to Deal with Parents of Students

The most common representation of this relationship is that of the Master-Servant, where the teacher is the Master and the parents are at their mercy as they are worried about the repercussions on their kid should they cross with the teacher. This applies to most of the private schools in the State.

This template should change to a friendlier approach and the teachers should take extra attempt to understand each kid in their class and the kid's background so they can be more empathetic as they will be handling kids from various socio-economic classes and different levels of conflicts in the family. The idea is not to pry into their personal lives but to get an overall picture so we can understand why the kid is behaving in such a way and hence implement individually catered strategies to correct them. The private schools have become the most sought after. When parents were questioned about "Why they chose expensive private schools over free of cost government run schools, the uniform answer from the majority was –

1. <u>Better infrastructure:</u>
    This is indeed a matter of concern as many kids refrain from using the rest rooms as they are not

clean. They are not clean because they are short staffed and it is physically challenging for a few people to do the work of many. Apart from this, novel facilities and opportunities for Sports are limited. Some private schools have tie-ups with International educational institutions and hence children get better exposure.

2. <u>Fluency in English:</u>

    This is another pressing issue given the current globalization schemata where English has become the professional language of the wider public and corporates. Expertise and ease while conversing in English is a must if we are to compete in the international forums and secure our niche in the society. Kids in government run schools are definitely not as fluent as their counterparts in private schools because the teachers themselves are not fluent. This can be circumvented by ensuring the teachers (except those teaching Thamizh) who are appointed in all schools are fluent in spoken English as well.

I hope to make the selection process for appointing teachers to Government schools more stringent and changing the current teachers recruitment examination system to a more apt one thus adapting to the coming era which needs more broad minded socially responsible individuals who are passionate about sculpting the young minds to make them resilient happy people.

Once we focus on improving the quality of the teaching and curriculum, people will understand that fancy infrastructure of a school alone is not all that important to ensure successful future for our children.

Teachers should be encouraged to treat every parent with respect and dignity. The poor people are not treated with respect anywhere in this country and may our State be the first to bring about this change. Every child that you come across is a seed that has abundant potential and will express it when planted in fertile soil with ambient atmospheric conditions.

There are some parents who are over-bearing and over-protective of their kids and pick up a fight with the teachers at the drop of a hat. For example, if a child was scolded by their teacher for failing a test, the parents cannot tolerate the act and they come to voice out the stress that their child has undergone due to being corrected by the teacher. Parents should note that if children's mistakes are never pointed out, they will never get the opportunity to learn because we learn only when our mistakes are pointed out, or else we will continue making the same mistakes. Corrections can be made only if we acknowledge our mistakes and take pro-active measures to correct them.

In such scenarios, the parents must be made to attend parenting classes (because nobody taught them how to parent) where they are taught when to hold back the leash and when to let go. If parents were to pitch in for every short coming of their kids, then their kids will grow to become spineless creatures who always need someone to voice out their concerns and develop a dependent personality which impedes them from leading a life of free will and courage.

Especially for Parents

In psychiatry we have a term called, "The Schizophrenogenic Parent" which denotes one or both parents with certain qualities that increase the chances of their child developing schizophrenia. They are:

1. <u>Covertly narcissistic parents:</u> They do not have genuine love for their child but their love stems from an underlying need for ownership and possession. So, the child is given an importance but that is because of their subconscious belief "you are MY child, I AM important, so you are also important as a side effect of my importance". The child's needs and wants will not be prioritized, but an image of "I am such a selfless parent" will be put forth amidst all friends and family making the child feel that they are infact incredibly lucky to have such a parent. This creates a conflict in the child because the child in 100% of the cases will clearly spot a fake person but when all evidence around says the opposite, the child will be left with a confusion on what is reality and will start questioning his/her own judgement. This process is the same process that pans out in the formation of a "Delusion" which is one of the classical

symptoms of Schizophrenia. If we create this mental dissonance (முரண்பாடு) in the kid's mind from childhood, it will deepen the insecurities and may potentiate the development of more mental health issues in the future.

2. **Instilling guilt** by constantly comparing the comforts that the child is having as opposed to the hardships the parents endured; the child feels guilty and feels the need to prove themselves worthy of every penny that they spend. This activates the survival mode where they are in a constant need to prove their worth.

3. <u>Over protective and over intrusive nature:</u> These parents believe that they have to live their child's life – if their child has something bothering them, they are compelled to bring themselves into the problem and solve it, all while constantly complaining and reassuring the kids at the same time. This makes the kids to develop like those "Bungalow Dogs" which have low virility and cannot withstand adverse life situations. It can be fine for a Bungalow Dog because it is going to be in the bungalow forever, but when kids are given such luxurious lives with a bed of roses, they develop low resilience and succumb to the slightest of the pressures, because we cannot assure the same bed of roses to our kids for a lifetime as the lifespan of humans has been prolonged due to the advent of medical sciences and we (parents) may not be around all the time.

The most important lessons to be taught to our kids –

"*அச்சம் தவிர்*".

"*தாழ்ந்து நடவேல்*".

"*நையப் புடை*".

They should be encouraged to fight their battles themselves in a **just** way as much as they can and reach out to us if they fail. If they are never given an opportunity to brave through difficult circumstances, then they will always be under someone else's mercy who in the longer run, will tend to take advantage of their helplessness and play havoc with their life.

4. <u>Sarcasm and criticism</u>: These parents often ridicule their child or embarrass them in front of the others (friends/family) because they have an inner anger that they cannot express directly owing to their narcissistic tendency; so they share their' child's personal stories and comment upon their child jokingly while demeaning them. This is the special ingredient to manufacture kids with a "low self-esteem" as this behaviour instils in them the belief that their parent/ parents hate them, and that they cannot win over their parents' love despite trying so hard or being so "good". In the future, it is these kids who get entangled in toxic abusive relationships and run from one narcissist to another acting like a narcissist magnet.

5. <u>Focusing on their own emotions and not considering their child's feelings:</u> The common example is – "If you go to your friend's house, I will be anxious all the time about your safety, so you should not go anywhere, you should stay indoors under lock and I don't care if you are lonely and bored", despite not making any attempts to know their child's friends or their whole life entirely. I have known a patient (7 years girl), whose mother would secretly ask her, "What standard she was studying in?", when guests arrived home so she need not cut a sorry figure as a mother who did not even know which standard her child was in. We all may have different professional goals and may not be available all the time for our kids, but the kids should never be left to feel, "I don't have anyone to care for me".

6. Treating their child as an extension of themselves and not as a separate individual who has their own set of feelings and thoughts.

7. They are cold and emotionless to their children and do not have reciprocal communication.

Financial Literacy

This is a skipped subject in all schools. Children are taught "Civics" but they seldom have a civic sense. What is the point of selling textbooks and making our kids memorize random facts and dates which prove to be absolutely useless? We all are aware of the fact that education does not make a person/child wise. It is agreed throughout the world. This is because what is necessary for life and what really matters is not taught in the classrooms. We can change this narrative by teaching things that matter and skipping the facts of the Balkans. In order to educate them about handling money, they should be taught what GST is, what are all the factors considered when it is set, who sets it, who are the beneficiaries, how to invest, the various investment schemes; and 25% of sanga ilakkiyam – students can read whatever chapters they are interested in and kaamathuppal of thirukkural (to gain emotional intelligence) etc., just to name a few. If all this is taught, then we can proudly say the Tamilnadu school education does make a person wise!

Economics, Data Science and Artificial Intelligence have promising careers in the future but are still unexplored in the Indian school curriculum. It is high time we revise the current curriculum in liaison with experts in the respective fields and impart knowledge to our kids, so they turn productive without having to spend a fortune on College education. Instead of spending rigorous 3-4 years geographically anchored to a particular location, they can spend their prime 20s (I consider the 20s as prime years because of physical agility and the rapid healing mechanism of the body in the earlier ages) travelling and gaining new experiences and meeting new people which would expand their opportunities professionally and on a spiritual level. You become the best version of yourself when you understand why another person is behaving the way they do, and accept them unconditionally without any judgement or discrimination. Sounds a lot like love, doesn't it?

Sex Education and Abuse

This entails a scientific description of what is sex, the importance of consent and protection; and whom to stay away from.

What is sex?

The process where in a hard (erect) penis of man/ transman penetrates into the vagina/anus of a woman/ transwoman/man/transman. This may or may not result in pregnancy. These are the acts that are usually considered to be "forbidden" and "sinful" by the conservative society if done before marriage. If the people/partners involved in this act are not planning a pregnancy, the following must be taught to them so they can have a healthy sexual relationship.

1. <u>Consent</u> – both the partners involved in it must be consenting to perform the act, it must NOT BE FORCED. If the woman/ or either partner says, "I'm not sure", or *"எனக்கு பயமா இருக்கு"*, the act should be curtailed immediately and the other partner should not force/manipulate/coerce the person to comply. The interested partner should wait for days/months/years or whatever it takes for their partner to be ready wholeheartedly. If the fear is pathological, they can seek therapy.

2. Teenagers should be taught that anything they do in secrecy may be recorded by the other partner and they should be ready to face dire consequences should they arise.

3. <u>They should be taught about sexually transmitted infections</u> – HIV, AIDS, Syphilis, Hepatitis B etc. and must be educated that some of these conditions need life-long medications. They can be shown pictures of people with the said conditions, so kids gain knowledge about the hazards of promiscuity (the habit of having sex with random strangers whose physical health condition is not known) and are quite careful about whom they have relationships with. They can get themselves tested but we cannot rely on the test done in August to hold good until September. The best advice for them is to always use protection – they should be encouraged to use condoms, which are widely available in all medical shops.

4. They need not comply to any unnatural act that is forced upon them by a dominant male/female. Any such attempts by perpetrators should be reported and it is a punishable offence.

Sexual Harassment

Harassment means "தொல்லை" in Thamizh.

Any act/message/call done by one person on another person which is not liked by this "another person" is termed a harassment. When this act pertains to a sexual context, it is termed a sexual harassment. It can be in the form of "spend time alone with me after dinner", or "come to my room, we can watch movie alone"... etc. The list is endless. You will be surprised at the number of sexual harassments that are happening in schools and colleges to girls/women/boys/men in this country.

The characteristics of sexual harassers

1. Invariably, most of them are boys/males. Sometimes females are also accused.

2. They are people in their late 30s to early 60s. This range in age is because of the age at which people enter and exit workforce. Once into their mid to late 30s, men ascend in their career and take advantage of their post and seniority. The upper limit was found to be early 60s in most of the observed data because of the retirement age which is 60 in most government and private institutions/offices.

3. These men are usually dissatisfied with their jobs, living a wretched life and have no meaningful relationships. The only meaning they have in their life is the pursuit of naïve women and coercing them into having affair with them which gives them a sense of "conquest". This is a reflection of underlying lack of masculinity and worthlessness; and very low dopamine reserves in the brain.

4. They have low self-love which will be evident in their unmaintained physical and mental health. They will not have a fitness regime, booze

regularly which further attenuates their physical health.

Like I have said before "Prevention is better than cure" – the best we can do is educate our girl children:

1. I hate to say this, but I tell all my female students "Always believe the rumours", when it comes to gossips about boys/men who have a past record of harassing women or misbehaving with them. Never give them the benefit of doubt. They should stay away from such predators as much as they can. Safety should be our primary concern, and it is better to be safer than sorry. Many a times, the victims of sexual harassment being young girls/women are scared to raise their voice against the harasser and suffer in silence venting out to their near and dear.

2. Be bold and talk back. Such harassers are usually narcissists who lack a sense of cohesive self and are constantly seeking external validation. If a girl makes a scene at the first hint of "Inappropriate Behaviour" the harasser will not dare repeat that behaviour. I know I am placing huge responsibility on women regarding their safety, but what else can we possibly do? Unless a law is passed where the harassers are given a punishment – which is severe enough to scare the perpetrators of the aftermath, harassment against women is going to continue in this country.

How do these harassers select their victims?

Victims are usually from low socio-economic status, with parents who are farmers or soft-spoken anxious people who will not create a scene, should anything deleterious happen.

Apart from this, the most important factor which these harassers bank on is "naivety" of young girls.

Girls/women who are bold, loud, courageous, have a political or other affluent background, are considered a "threat" by these harassers and they make conscious efforts to not disturb them. Among these factors, the most important aspect of women that harassers were put off by was found to be women who are "Bold and Loud". I would like to quote what actress Priyanka Chopra said in one of her interviews:

"Good girls don't make history, Bold girls do", – You need not even make history, just stay alive – for yourself and for a 100 more other girls to come.

Good Touch and Bad Touch

The teachings of "Good Touch and Bad Touch" have become popular in schools these days and it is indeed a great step ahead in instilling "Boundaries" in young minds.

Let me start by telling you a story:

He was 44 years old. Her name is Kuzhali and she (8 years old) called him uncle. After her lessons on "Good

Touch and Bad Touch" in school, she put forth her stand very clear in the house and also educated all the other women in the family on what was taught. She was the brightest student in class and her family encouraged her to implement such things taught in school. Her uncle (father's younger brother) who would stay in her house often was alarmed at this as this was the first time he was hearing such "Boundaries". He initially paid no heed to her words and pulled her closer to him and made her sit on his lap by force. She started screaming and this drew all her family members to the spot. Later, she was calmed down by her mother, the uncle was told to respect her boundaries and the situation was settled.

What was taught in school?

<u>Good Touch</u> – shaking hands, high-fives, pats on the back, any touch that does not make you feel uncomfortable.

<u>Bad Touch</u> – makes you feel uncomfortable, touching private parts, lips, pinching, hitting etc.

This uncle was alarmed because she did not let him –

(i) pull her by force,
(ii) draw her bottom and pull her towards his lap,
(iii) kiss her on the cheeks.

This is what most "uncles" do in this country. Even I was disgusted by one such uncle who kissed me on the cheeks against my wish when I was 9 years old.

As Kuzhali was very particular about this "Touch", her uncle just kept to high-fiving her and giving her a bear hug whenever he needed to express his love or excitement to her.

This is how the turn of events will be in a healthy family. If it turns otherwise, then these touches will soon culminate in rapes sooner than you think.

You may think, "What is there in a touch?".

The perpetrators of rape: Are usually men who are well known to the family, they are trusted by the kids' parents blindly and in dire circumstances the parents don't even believe it when their daughter tells them that such an "Uncle" has touched her inappropriately. These perpetrators follow and study the child like a project, they master the child's daily routine, and as they are well aware of the parents' capabilities and to what extent they will resort to seek justice, they plunge into action and from there on, we all know how their plan unfolds.

I would like to highlight the point that -

"All bad touch, at first begins with GOOD TOUCH".

Does Everyone Deserve Kids?

To be honest, nobody who has ever lived or lives now has the right or audacity to answer this question. In life we would have come across countless circumstances where we thought for a split second, "This person doesn't deserve to have kids".

Why is this a topic of discussion?

I was called over to the Emergency Department to assess a 17 years old girl because she attempted to kill herself. She jumped from the fourth floor of her apartment building and sustained fracture to her hip and was bedridden.

She was admitted in the Emergency Ward and as I was talking to the mother, she said, "Doctor, I don't have leave, I am a Higher Secondary Teacher and I have to complete portions... You know the Board Exams are nearing and I cannot take leave now as I am the senior teacher. You please take care of her", and she sprinted even before I could process what she said.

It was at that split second, I thought – "Some people don't deserve kids"—but before I could dwell on it – the following story panned out.

<u>The patient's story</u>: "I grew up all alone. Amma was never around. If I need food, she will just give me money

and ask me to buy them from the canteen. My younger sister and I were always left to fend for ourselves emotionally. I felt very lonely even as child. There was nobody for me. At school, I had a friend who was very nice to me. He used to bring chocolates, help me do my homework, and also accompany me to tuition. He told me that he will take care of me and he will give me all the care and affection that I deserved. After few months he said he loved me and promised to marry me. So, I accepted his proposal and we had sex. After that happened, he stopped talking to me. I felt as if the whole world came crashing towards me. He was the only person for me whom I could call "Mine" and when he left, I couldn't take it. I begged him to talk to me, but he blocked me. There is no reason for me to be alive. Nobody would even care if I died. My grandparents may cry for a while but they will forget. It is enough for me if he just talks to me...".

<u>When asked about her parents</u>: "Amma was always working and even in the few hours when she was home, she was studying. I don't have any memory of my father. I have seen him only in photos".

<u>Her back story</u>: Her father was involved in Business and had no time for family. He was always working, travelling etc. Her mother who was married to her father against her will when she was only 16 years of age has been having a painful marital life. Her mother was not educated at the time of marriage, and she did not think that that was possible for someone from her family as all

the women in her family were housewives and the men were the bread winners. She too expected the same when she was married and sent off to live with her in-laws. Her husband who was a respected man in his community was 15 years older than her and the maximum purpose she had in his life was to bear his children according to him. He treated her exactly as a baby making machine, making her yield to his sexual pleasures and fantasies. He was and is addicted to alcohol. Even before the mother could figure out things, she had two girl children. As both the kids were girls, and girls were considered as a burden in the socio-political status that they came from, the father harassed his wife and raped her several times as he believed that, "If a child is conceived by force, the increased energy used will manifest in the conception of a male baby". The mother could not endure all this suffering wrought at her and she decided to leave the household with her two kids – aged 5 and 3. With the help of her parents, she got BA, MA, B.Ed., (educational degrees) and with her grit and determination she secured her place as a permanent Government School Teacher. She was very hardworking, sincere and did the best she can to help poor students and prevented many young girls from dropping out of school as there was a custom of getting girls married soon after puberty.

The mother's story is an exceptionally inspiring story of valour and alphaness!

But what happened to the children?

The children become the collateral damage of all such broken and disrupted families/couples. Here I would like to thank our Ex and current Chief Ministers who are striving hard to eradicate starvation from the grass root levels to promote education but more emphasis on mental well-being is also needed.

Every story has two sides. I have told you both the sides. Now I have a few questions to ask:

1. What could have prevented the girl from wanting to kill herself?
2. What could have made her boyfriend give her "princess treatment" until they had sex and then break up with her?
3. What could have made her mother abandon her children and prioritise work?
4. What could have made her father treat women as "child bearing machines"?
5. Why were her parents married to each other in the first place?
6. Why did her father and all the men in the family were the sole bread winners?
7. Why were all the women in her family living as housewives? Was it their personal choice or was it imposed upon?
8. When the mother was married off at 16, why was she not able to voice out her displeasure about the marriage?

Now you tell me – "Does everyone deserve kids?" – Is this a rational or an irrational question?

Adoption

Given the rise in the number of "Fertility centers" across the country, it is becoming more evident that many couples are infertile and are unable to beget children due to a lot of health issues. This is a matter of serious concern because we can witness the drop in the birth rates from our grandparents' generation who easily had 4-5 children to the current generation parents where giving birth to a single healthy child has come to be a wonderful stroke of luck. There are many biological reasons among which inflammation and stress play the leading role according to experts. Inflammation is triggered by the junk food that is widely available and we are consuming such foods on an everyday basis which was considered to be an occasional delicacy 50 years ago.

Given this background where couples are unable to have kids, they are now spending a fortune for conception and practically lose all their life's earnings on special hormonal injections and finally when they do conceive, they are almost bankrupt and have no money to afford a healthy lifestyle and education for the kid. When you are planning to receive a child, it doesn't end with healthy pregnancy and delivery alone. We may not be able to control and curate our child's entire life ahead, but we need to ascertain the availability of care and the financial means to attain it to a certain extent, lest the whole struggle that one has underwent to beget a child turns pointless.

That being said, I would like to quote -

"பெற்றால் தான் பிள்ளையா?"

Having a biological child is a dream for many people, but if that becomes a herculean task, why not consider adoption?

Pros of adoption

1. It gives immense sense of pleasure and gratitude.
2. You feel magnanimous (பெருந்தன்மை மிக்க) and experience abundance.
3. You have planted a seed, which in future may eradicate famine and drought for the greater population.

Cons of adoption

1. My professor used to say, "You have to analyse why does a child end up in an orphanage?" – I don't mean to demean the characteristics of the child, but would like to throw light on the personality traits of the parents. Most of the biological parents of children who ended up in orphanages had alcohol addiction, anti-social personality traits.
2. These children were mostly conceived out of wedlock and this reflects the irresponsibility and the lack of accountability on the parents' part. Had

they had healthy bio-psycho-social parameters themselves, they would not have let the child to its own fate.

3. Such children unfortunately harbour the genetic make ups of their parents and may develop the same characteristics of their biological parents. The role that the genes play in developing mental illness and character has been proved by several studies that have concluded that "Most of the (but not all) adopted away offsprings of alcohol addicts grew up to become addicted to alcohol themselves", despite growing in entirely different, safe, healthy environments.

4. Parents who adopt a child may feel guilty while disciplining them as they have this subconscious thought – "Would have I done this to my own child?" Due to this, some adopted children are pampered and grow up to become arrogant and narcissistic adults who pose a unique set of problems to themselves and to those around them.

All that said, "How interesting would your life be, if you are going to be living the same day everyday?

A little bit of randomness can add spice to life, but are you ready to deal with it?

The choice is entirely up to each individual to make. As an expert in behavioural sciences, I have detailed the pros and cons of adoption and I am not recommending this unless the parents are ready to commit.

How to Understand the Mind and Human Emotions?

The human mind has never ceased to fascinate the scholars since time immemorial. There are several ancient texts that have elaborated on the mind and its various functions. For any novice reader I would suggest to read the following in the same order:

(i) <u>My previous book</u> – Buy Happiness from a Bookshelf, available on Amazon. This book details on why people behave the way they do and is a very good start on your journey towards understanding yourself and those around you. This explains the mind from the Western and Eastern perspectives thereby catering to everyone in this era making it the "Go to" book for self-discovering happiness.

(ii) <u>Thirukkural (திருக்குறள்)</u> – by Thiruvalluvar (kindly read the explanation given by many authors. There is a website – thirukkural.ai which has all the detailed versions).

(iii) Thirumandhiram (திருமந்திரம்).

(iv) Agananooru (அகநானூறு).

(v) <u>Tholkappiyam</u> – porul adhigaaram (தொல்காப்பியம் பொருள் அதிகாரம்).

The Unfortunate Fate of the Future Generation and New Problems – The Second Hit

Why am I calling them unfortunate?

80% of the world we see around us is the perfectly decorated version of people's lives that they want to be shown to the world outside.

The clothes that the people wear, the phones that they use, the cars they drive, the high rise apartment they live in, etc. are the external vices that are discernible. What we don't know is:-

(i) <u>The clothes that the people wear</u> – *"The fight they had with their spouse that morning while dressing up"*.

(ii) <u>The phones that they use</u> – *"What they actually speak about in their phones"*.

(iii) <u>The cars they drive</u> – *"The tears they shed in isolation while in the car"*.

(iv) <u>The high-rise apartment they live in</u> – *"The unending EMI that they have to pay"*.

The detrimental effect that this has on our current generation is the excessive preoccupation over one's physical appearance and external attributes. The ideal of beauty which was once defined as having a lighter skin tone is no longer worshipped upon, but now the ideal of beauty has moved towards having a fit body, flawless skin, chiseled face etc.

The most disabling of all these is the perceived flaw in one's facial features, because if you want to change any of your facial features it is going to cost you a fortune and the odds are that even after the "Corrective Surgery" you may or may not be satisfied with the outcome. This preoccupation with external beauty is becoming commoner as days progress, due to the "Easy and Overnight rise to Popularity" by the common people who have portrayed themselves to be attractive.

In the adolescent period, focusing on one's self image is a natural part of biological development but how much of this "Focus" is allowed?

<u>This focus is considered to be pathological if it:</u>

- (i)   causes any disturbance in the child's academics,
- (ii)   disrupts the child's social life wherein some children refuse to leave their rooms because they believe that everyone would make fun of their appearance,
- (iii)   makes them spend excess time in front of the mirror, take hours to get ready, use special make ups/sunglasses to hide their perceived flaws,

(iv)   makes them irritable and easily triggered causing outbursts of intense anger.

Why is this recent trend "I want to look beautiful" happening?

Like I have mentioned in previous chapters, adolescence is the phase where we strive to create an identity for ourselves.

The questions of "Who am I? What is my worth?" keep knocking on the brain's doors incessantly.

As on date, a person's worth is largely assessed upon the "Good Lookingness" of a person and the number of followers they have on Instagram. Fortunately, "Material Wealth" is slowly losing its importance as one of the criteria to assess one's worth. 20-30 years ago, one's worth was directly proportional to the amount of money they had.

Why has this "Self-worth / Self-esteem" largely become to be dictated upon by how a person looks?

Self-esteem (சுயமரியாதை) (the confidence and satisfaction in oneself) is monumental in shaping one's mind and it is the driving force for every individual to aspire to achieve their dreams. This is the building block on which all other emotions are levied upon, because in inter-personal interactions, our mind subconsciously assesses our self-worth and the opponent's worth and it is this balance that predicts the course of further conversation.

Many of you may find this hard to imagine, but think of the way you talk to your Building Watchman and your

Boss... (There are a few superior minded high vibrational people who treat everyone with respect, but they constitute only a small fraction).

For example, I know someone who occupies the highest post in the institution but his level of pettiness is unmatchable. This is a real-life incident that happened to me.

Few years ago, while I was working in a Medical College, I was invited by a neighboring college to deliver a lecture on "Mental Health at Workplace", note the irony! As the time allocated to the speech was within the working hours of the Medical College that I was working in, I needed authorized permission from the Institution. Hence, I requested the other College Principal to send an email to me and my Boss, so it doesn't cause any confusion.

But can you guess what my Boss was offended by with? In the email, my email id was written in the "To" and my Boss's email was "CC"d. This was his only problem. He proclaimed that, "The email should have been sent to me and CC'd to you".

In this fast-paced world, and among his 1000 duties and problems, he decided to make this as his 1001st problem. Why?

This is where self-esteem comes into play. The way you treat the others depends on how much you love and respect yourself. If you don't respect yourself enough, you will start desperately seeking respect and validation from the whole world around you and sometimes even demanding it. You will respect yourself when you consider yourself worthy. This self-worth/ self-esteem comes from a personal sense of accomplishment. To get this "Accomplishment" you should have actually accomplished something that is of value and purpose to you i.e., (it should make sense to you, not to prove to others).

Self-esteem or self-worth is hard to attain through Intellectual means (through education/research/ etc.). This requires hard work, persistence, determination, consistency and an unquenching thirst to seek answers to questions that makes us sleepless. However, it is relatively easier to camouflage your pimple scars and draw your eyebrows. In other words, it has become easier to maintain self-esteem and self-worth through "Maintaining a standard of physical appearance" than to maintain self-esteem through academic or financial accomplishment.

This is why "How I look" is becoming a pressing issue of concern in today's age. I do not mean to speak of "Make up products" in a derogatory manner; it is an art form, and I have immense respect for art.

Preoccupation with having a fit body is not bad because when a healthy high fibre diet and exercise regime is incorporated into the daily life, along with a fit body also comes a healthy mind and a flawless skin. The side effects of this preoccupation are also useful and hence that is not considered a pathology unless it causes impairment which needs therapeutic intervention.

When does this become a pathology?

When a bunch of 15 years old boys (who initially aspired to become Doctors and Engineers in IIT) spend 3 hours a day in the gym wanting to achieve a "chiseled" face it is quite concerning. Spending 3 hours in the gym is not a crime, if you want to become a model or compete in the body building championship tournament; but it is a criminal waste of time if you have the ambition of becoming a doctor or want to enter IIT.

How is this related to mental illness?

In psychiatry we have something called "The Second Hit" or the most dangerous hit.

For example, a person born to parents with Diabetes has an increased chance of developing Diabetes in the future. This is the "First Hit". If that person has a sedentary lifestyle, consumes junk food, drinks alcohol and smokes, he/she will become a Diabetic soon. The factors described above constitute what we call "The Second Hit".

Getting the "First Hit" is inevitable (தவிர்க்க முடியாதது) because we don't decide who our parents are going to be; but we can decide the "Second Hit" because in this case – having a healthy lifestyle, eating vegetables, working out, not drinking or smoking are entirely in our hands as adults and hence the "Second Hit" can be prevented from happening 90% of the times in case of adult onset diseases. It is quite challenging to prevent the "Second Hit" from happening during childhood because the parents have to be extremely perceptive and knowledgeable about health and wellness for them to inculcate certain practices in their home. We cannot be taking responsibility for things that are beyond our control.

Applying the same concept to mental illness, the "First Hit" happens when we inherit the risky genes from our parents. We don't control this. In most cases we are not even aware of this. Risky genes don't necessarily mean your parents had the disease. They may have the genes that are not expressed, so they become the "Silent Carriers", sometimes they may become ill and suffer from the illness; Who may or may not develop the disease – Nobody really knows.

You may ask if genes are entirely or partly responsible for mental health conditions why not get it tested or try gene replacement therapies?

(i)   Genes are only partly responsible for the development of mental illness.

(ii) Mental illness is not the result of expression of one faulty gene but the cumulative expression of multiple faulty/different genes. The presence of all faulty genes also does not guarantee the future evolution of mental illness. For example, between two individuals K and J harboring the genes for Bipolar Disorder – K can become terribly ill while J can become the greatest poet this world has seen. This is the tricky part while handling mental health conditions.

What is the "Second Hit" in mental illness and when does it happen?

Between K and J having the same genes that increases their risk of developing Bipolar Disorder, K's Bipolar genes are expressed explicitly while J's is protected from developing the disease. Why?

K – Had a rough traumatic childhood, no parental love or protection, left to deal with life by herself.

J – Had a loving childhood, parents were around most of the time to cater to J's emotional needs, had reciprocal interaction and affection with parents.

Despite all the damage control that current day parents are striving to provide for their children, the damage done during childhood is unsalvageable, thereby leading to the metamorphosis of a diseased mind with unstable emotions predicting a life with medications for a lifetime.

The "Second Hit" in this case described above is – the lack of parental support in K's life.

In current day and age how is the "Second Hit" influenced by social media?

The "Second Hit" is determined by different indices for different illnesses. Given the current technological revolution, we cannot give a blind eye to its influence on the youth.

<u>The First Hit</u> – This leads to certain disturbances in the functioning of the brain which may become

pronounced during adolescence. These disturbances manifest themselves depending on each individual's socio-economic-political situations which together constitute the "Second Hit".

For example, let us say a child named K has a genetic vulnerability to develop mental illness.

Situation 1: If K is brought up in a healthy environment with adequate stimulation and right food, then K can escape from receiving the Second Hit.

Situation 2: If K is brought up in a neglected manner, no stimulation, this becomes the "Second Hit" to trigger the development of mental illness.

Given this era, where social media plays undue role in shaping one's life and personality, the "Second Hit" is almost always due to something the child saw or heard on the phone.

The Second Hit – varies for each kid. For example, there was a 14 year old girl who already had a "First Hit", but she was absolutely alright, being the topper of her class until one day she randomly saw a picture of a male private part while scrolling YouTube. Since then, she has been getting repeated flashes of that image in her mind and it was extremely distressing for her. She was started on medications and made significant improvement.

I would like to make it clear that not every child seeing pictures on the internet would develop mental illness.

This child who has already gotten the "First Hit" is more at risk. It is pertinent to have a psychiatrist assess school kids periodically to ensure "High Risk" children get more attention.

How is low self-esteem related to the Second Hit?

Another "Second Hit" that is becoming common is – "The need to look beautiful". This need springs up from a low self-esteem which kids tend to compensate by giving excess attention to the way they look so they can boost their morale. There is a child S, who had excess preoccupation with the way he looked and he even cut his face with a blade because he wanted a sharp jawline. Before we judge "Today's kids" we should understand the extent of distractions and the level of distress these kids face in today's world. They can no longer buy their own house with their single income. Making a mark for themselves is going to get harder and harder. Let us cut them a little slack and be kind to them.

In such cases, identifying the kids with "First Hit" will go a long way in preventing the disease burden and ensure that even kids with high risk for mental illness can lead lives as per their wish and not a life being a victim of their genes.

Low self-esteem can be overcome by encouraging kids to excel in either academics or any other vocational study of their choice. When they have a good self-esteem which is achieved through intellectual means, then they will stop paying attention to the "external beauty" as a means to maintain self esteem. This is healthier in the long run because the "physical appearance" is something that fades away with time, the aging process is going to give us wrinkles, cause greying of hair etc. In such cases, the level of self-esteem will tend to fluctuate causing disruption to their personal and professional life. On the other hand, if self-esteem is achieved and maintained through **"Intellectual"** means, then aging will only increase the intellectual potential and such individuals will grow to become more resilient and contented than the others.

Physical appearances will fade away with time but the intellect ages like fine wine.

Hence it is wise to invest on the "Intellect" so we can get guaranteed Returns than on "Physical Appearance" the value of which depreciates with time.

Respect and Sanatana Dharma

This still had to be a topic of discussion because of the current socio-political situation.

Children are expected to blindly obey elders and express respect in the form of "Body Language" which has its roots in Sanatana Dharma. I will list it down for the readers to come to a conclusion themselves.

<u>Most of us were:</u>

(i)   Not allowed to wear proper clothes,

(ii)   Not allowed to wear slippers while crossing the streets where members of the upper caste lived,

(iii)   Not allowed to sit in a chair- we either had to stand or sit outside of the class,

(iv)   Not allowed to speak out loud or have an opinion etc.

Fast forward to 2025, even today, in some villages the members of a particular caste are not allowed to sit in a chair during meetings and they keep standing throughout the meetings.

Now come to today – We believe that children are respectful when they rise from their chairs when an adult enters their midst, when they nod "Yes" to everything that was told to them, speak softly, tolerate disrespect etc.

What is the latest definition of respect?

Respect is when someone values your time, likes and dislikes. Plain and simple.

The changes in body language that is expected of everyone will make us go back in our evolution where we purposely did purposeless things.

Respect yourself and the others around you.

Is Information Wealth?

If you are a 90s kid, you might remember the role played by actor Senthil in the movie "BOYS" by Director Shankar. He would have the entire schedule of "anna dhaanam" (அன்னதானம்) in all the temples in Chennai with the exact dates and time. With this information he would live happily on the temple premises with no worry of how he is going to get food on his plate because he has gotten all the necessary "Database" which would enable him to lead a worriless and penniless life.

We would have learnt in our school days that "Knowledge is Wealth".

<u>Both these concepts</u> – "Information and Knowledge" don't differ much from each other. These concepts did hold good in the olden days when Internet was not in our hands and everything that was to know about the world had to be stored in our brains through reading and memorizing. Through the vast amount of Information we stored in our brains we were able to make a decent living – this would explain why doctors made good money 20-30 years ago.

Given this date and age, every information or data is at our fingertips and we can gain access to practically any range of information ranging from what is happening in our neighbour's house to what is happening in the NASA.

Hence "Information" no longer leads to "Wealth". Now, it is Technology and the new ideas that can possibly amass wealth. If we want our kids to grow both intellectually and materially, then they must be encouraged to study Thamizh and Computers.

The Importance of Reducing School Dropouts

It is with pride we can say that the Primary school enrollment in Tamilnadu is one of the highest in the country. In Tamilnadu, the enrollment of children in Primary schools is much higher compared to their enrollment in Middle and Higher Secondary schools. There are many social and economic reasons for the reduction in Middle and Higher Secondary school enrollment.

The psychological aspects of this alone is discussed here

Children with any mental health issue can easily cope up with the syllabus in the Primary Schools as their brain is developing and can be adaptable to minor challenges. Upon entering the Middle schools, the curriculum is quite vast and those brains that are not able to handle the load in the syllabus tend to drop out.

This can be understood from the following evidence:

1. 92% of patients with psychosis diagnosed in their early twenties had a poor academic history.
2. They have not been able to secure any kind of employment due to their deficiencies in cognition (அறிவாற்றல்).

3. They were all considered to be "Dull Students" and hence were thought to have "No Interest" in studies.

4. Only 25% of the patients with psychosis had passed their 10th standard Board exams with a score of "just pass".

Explanation

Certain mental health conditions like "psychosis", "depression" etc. manifests itself initially with "reduced cognition".

Cognition is a set of functions of the brain that encompasses the processes of :-

(i) Attention

(ii) Perception

(iii) Learning

(iv) Memory

(v) Thinking

(vi) Analysing

(vii) Decision making

(viii) Judgement

(ix) Planning

When we think of someone having a certain "mental illness", we immediately think that they will be someone acting "crazy" or "weird". It is not always so. These "crazy" or "weird" states of mind tend to appear later in the course of the illness. The **beginning stages** of mental illness will usually be a **"failed academic record"**.

It is necessary to assess all the school dropouts and screen them for the presence of any mental health issues. If such children are identified and given adequate treatment and therapy, then the dropouts due to mental illness will largely be reduced; once they are treated, the children themselves will demand to be sent to school. This will reduce the burden of mental illness in the country.

People with mental illness (who were not identified in their early stages) live a life with QoL index (value measuring the quality of life) that is 3 standard deviations below the Qol of their mentally healthy siblings and other members of their cohort. This means that if a child is not identified in their early stages of mental illness, then they will be forced to live a miserable life where they are completely dependent upon another family member or the government for their basic food and shelter.

In Thamizh, families of people with untreated mental illness are perfectly described as "வாழ்ந்து கெட்ட குடும்பம்".

About the Author

Dr Kaviya Thamizhi was born in a middle class family and strived her way up the academic ladder. She has completed her MBBS from KAPV Government Medical college in Trichy, MD in psychiatry from Institute of Mental Health (Madras Medical College) in India, then went on to obtain MRCPsych from Royal College of Psychiatrists in London. Post this, she worked in the Adult Community Mental health Clinic in Birmingham and then moved back to India as she realised her calling was more than just amassing wealth. She is also a certified Yoga Therapist from Yoga Alliance USA. She holds a Black belt in Karate and occasionally teaches Karate to school kids in her spare time.

Currently she practices in her Clinic in Villupuram.

Owing to her deep passion and நசைன for Thamizh and her inspiration from Thamizh literature, she changed her surname to Thamizhi.

Thirukkural, Tholkappiyam, Bharathiyar kavithaigal are some of her favourite reads.

Her childhood was turbulent and as an adult she has made it her life's purpose to bring up happy children and that is the seed for this book to blossom and flourish.

In her own words – "While travelling through this book, I have made amends with my mother, something that I thought was impossible."

As she is extensively trained in Western Medicine and the Western concept of Psychiatry, her passion for Thamizh literature and interest in the Eastern concepts gave her a new perspective on "Mind" and this helped her to bring her patients to recovery faster.

Her first book – "Buy Happiness from a Bookshelf with a 21 days inner exploration program" published in 2021 was critically acclaimed by experts and serves as the "Go to" guide for a happy soulful life. This book was published under her official name Kaviya Balasubramanian.

Insta handle: dr_kaviyathamizhi_psychiatrist

இந்நூல் – சிதைக்கப்பட்ட என் குழந்தைப்
பருவத்தை மீட்க கோரி